Tips and Traps
When
Buying a Home

Other McGraw-Hill Books by Robert Irwin

Tips and Traps When Buying a Home

Fourth Edition

ROBERT IRWIN

New York   Chicago   San Francisco   Lisbon   London   Madrid   Mexico City
Milan   New Delhi   San Juan   Seoul   Singapore   Sydney   Toronto

The McGraw·Hill Companies

1 2 3 4 5 6 7 8 9 0   FGR/FGR   0 1 5 4 3 2 1 0 9 8

ISBN   978–0–07–150841–4
MHID   0–07–150841–4

This publication is designed to provide accurate and authoritative information in regard to the subject matter covered. It is sold with the understanding that neither the author nor the publisher is engaged in rendering legal, accounting, futures/securities trading, tax, or other professional service. If legal advice or other expert assistance is required, the services of a competent professional person should be sought.

—*From a Declaration of Principles jointly adopted by a Committee of the American Bar Association and a Committee of Publishers*

AUTHOR'S NOTE: Laws and regulations that affect the buying, selling, financing, and taxation of real estate are from time to time passed, changed, or amended by federal or state governments. Therefore, check with a real estate professional before taking action on real estate to see how this could affect you.

REALTOR® is a registered collective membership mark which may be used only by real estate professionals who are members of the NATIONAL ASSOCIATION OF REALTORS® and subscribe to its strict Code of Ethics.

McGraw-Hill books are available at special quantity discounts to use as premiums and sales promotions, or for use in corporate training programs. To contact a representative, please visit the Contact Us pages at www.mhprofessional.com.

This book is printed on acid-free paper.

Library of Congress Cataloging-in-Publication Data

Irwin, Robert.
    Tips and traps when buying a home / by Robert Irwin.—4th ed.
        p. cm.
    Includes bibliographical references and index.
    ISBN 0–07–150841–4 (alk. paper)
1. House buying. 2. Real estate business. I. Title.
    HD1379.I67 2009
    643'.12—dc22   2008022923

Contents

Preface

How do you get the best home in the best location for the best price in any market?

How do you avoid expensive problems in a purchase before they can occur?

This latest edition of *Tips and Traps When Buying a Home* gives you sound suggestions on finding the right home, getting a good price, finding a foreclosure, dealing with agents, spotting home defects, negotiating, understanding contracts and closings, and all the other complex issues associated with a home purchase regardless of market conditions. It points out the traps to avoid and gives you helpful tips so that your buying experience will be pleasurable and rewarding.

Who Should Read This Book?

This book is especially designed for you:

 If you want an exceptional deal

 If you're searching for a foreclosure

 If you're moving up or downsizing

 If you're buying for investment

 If you're buying a brand new home

 If you're a first-time buyer

Tips and Traps When Buying a Home will give you tips that will benefit you as a buyer as well as point to the traps that can ensnare the unwary. It will show you how to make a successful and profitable purchase, even your first time out.

Is This the Right Time to Buy?

Is there a right time to buy a home? Is there a wrong time?

Actually, the answer to both questions is, "Yes!"

Here's your first tip. The best time to buy a home is in the winter, around New Year's Day.

Why? The reason is that most people are busy with holidays at year's end. There are presents to buy and parties to organize and go to. Besides, the weather is usually terrible and people tend to want to just be home in front of a fire.

Most people want things to be stable. The holidays are traumatic enough without any big changes occurring. Hence, the last thing they want to do is buy . . . or sell a home.

That means that there are fewer buyers out there—your competition is greatly diminished. Further, those sellers who do keep their homes on the market tend to be those who must sell, who are desperate to sell.

Thus, at year's end you have a combination of fewer buyers and highly motivated sellers—what could be a better time to make a purchase?! It's the perfect bargain hunting time.

Further, the deadest week of the year is between Christmas and New Year's Day. Nobody wants to be out there worrying about real estate. Yet I've made the best real estate purchases of my life during that week.

TIP

The best time to buy is at the end of the year.

The corollary to this is that the worst time to buy is late spring and early summer. That's when people with families are out there looking so they can move during summer when the kids are not at school. There are more buyers and more competition than any other time of the year.

Sellers see all that attention and hold to their prices. Hence, you're likely to get the worst deal.

What About When Prices Are Falling . . . or Rising?

Here's your second tip.

When there's a real estate recession and prices are falling, hold off from buying as long as you can.

It only makes sense. Whatever you pay for your property today, chances are it will be worth less tomorrow. Thus, there's no advantage in buying quickly—waiting usually pays off with a lower price to you.

Many people who sell their homes during a period of falling prices and then want to buy, temporarily rent. Yet, by renting they lose the benefits of ownership:

Tax and interest deductions off their taxes

Security

Privacy

However, they gain the benefit of buying a home at a lower price.

On the other hand, when prices are rising, you want to get into the market and buy as soon as possible. That way you lock in a price and ride the wave to higher equity values.

TIP

When prices fall, wait to buy. When prices are rising, buy as soon as you can.

Of course, there's a trap here. It's that almost no one, including the so-called experts, can predict the bottom or the top of any market. We only see it in hindsight. Thus, while waiting in a down market is a good idea, you don't want to wait too long.

TRAP

Don't try to catch the peak or the trough of the market. If you do, chances are you'll miss and be left behind.

What Type of Finance Should You Get?

The big questions about financing real estate are often, "When should you get an adjustable-rate mortgage (ARM)?" and "When should you get a fixed-rate mortgage?"

As those in the field know, the ARM's interest rate (and monthly payments) moves up and down depending on economic conditions. The fixed rate (and monthly payment), on the other hand, remains the same for the life of the loan.

Here's your tip—Get an ARM when interest rates are falling. That way your interest rate and your payments will fall as interest rates go down. Get a fixed rate when interest rates are rising. That way you lock in a low rate and low payment even though rates are rising all around you.

Get an ARM in a falling interest rate market and a fixed-rate mortgage in a rising interest rate market.

Once again, a warning goes with this tip. Today, most ARMs are hybrids of one sort or another. They combine an initial low interest rate (called a "teaser") fixed for a short time, often a year or two, with an adjustable rate for the remaining life of the mortgage.

The temptation is to get the ARM in *any market* in order to benefit from the teaser—the initial low rate. The problem is that while you may be able to afford the teaser, you may not be able to afford the final rate when the mortgage resets after a year or two. Thus, unless you can refinance or resell at the reset time, you could lose your home to foreclosure. This inability to refinance or sell is in large part what caused the mortgage crisis of 2007 and 2008.

TRAP

Don't get stung by a teaser.

What Is the Real Estate "Cycle"?

The poet and philosopher George Santayana said, "Those who cannot remember the past are condemned to repeat it." This has never been truer than in real estate.

During the brief "bubble" that lasted roughly between 1999 and 2006, most buyers acted as though real estate would forever go up in price. They seemed to believe that the housing market was the golden road to riches—that it always had and always would go up and up.

I used to question buyers during that period—I'd ask them if they remembered the last housing "bust," the one that occurred during the mid-1990s, only a few years earlier. I remember people looking at me as if I was from another planet. "Real estate prices don't go down," they scoffed, and moved on to make another bid.

Of course, more recently during the housing recession that started roughly in 2007, I'd ask people if they thought the market would soon turn around. Often they'd reply that it would be a very long time before houses would again go up in price, if ever. A common answer was, "We'll never see prices like that again."

What nonsense!

A quick read of real estate history reveals that since the Great Depression (few housing records were kept before the 1930s), the residential real estate market has moved up and down with almost clockwork precision. We've usually had 7 years of down or generally low markets often followed by 7 years of slowly rising or sometimes galloping markets—a 14-year cycle. (Remember the real estate recession of 1992–1999? And the previous boom phase of 1985–1992? And so on?)

Those savvy in the business often talk about the market changing every seven years. Some investors bet their hats on it.

No, there's no guarantee that this cycle will continue into the future. But, if you choose to ignore it, you do so at your peril.

Pay attention to the real estate cycle. Good and bad markets come and go . . . with surprising regularity.

Should You Buy at All?

How's your timing?

As we've seen, timing a purchase is important. But that sometimes leads to discouragement. It can too easily become a matter of thinking, "Maybe there's never a right time to purchase a home."

That's the biggest mistake you can make and the tip here is simply this: when you buy, watch out for:

- The time of the year
- Whether prices are rising or falling

- Whether you get an ARM or a fixed-rate loan
- Where you are in the real estate cycle

Yes, depending on how you read the above, you may want to wait a while. Or you may want to move more quickly. But don't throw the baby out with the bath water. Buying at some point almost always makes more sense than not buying.

When you buy a home, new or resale, you get the advantage of price appreciation over time, increased security, privacy, and tax benefits. Over 65 million homeowners in America can't be wrong.

What's Your Reason for Buying?

I s there a right reason to buy a home? Is there a wrong one?

People buy homes for all sorts of reasons, both good and bad. *Why* you're buying helps to determine *what* you should buy as well as how much you should spend.

In this chapter we'll look at the most common reasons for buying a home. Then we'll see how those translate into the home of your dreams.

Buying as an Investment

While this may not be the primary reason that most people would give for buying a home, it's the one reason that almost everyone includes on their list. Homes are simply too expensive these days not to consider their investment potential. Indeed, it's often pointed out that a home is usually a person's single biggest lifetime investment.

Since you're buying a home at least in part to make money, it only makes sense to be sure that your property fits the profile of a good investment. (Yes, unfortunately many properties are *not* good investments.) Therefore, what should you look for when your reason for buying is to maximize your profit?

TIP

Here's a big tip: The most important investment consideration when buying is how well the home will resell.

What?! Think about reselling before even buying?

Yes. We're now looking at the home from a business perspective. And here, the ability to sell the home for a profit is paramount. The rub comes from the fact that what makes a home resalable may not always be what we personally like best about it.

For example, the home you've found and like may have only two bedrooms. Since there's just two of you, you feel that's fine— there's even room for a guest room. You like the idea of a smaller, cozier space.

However, if you consider the broader spectrum of buyers, you'll find that very few want a two-bedroom house—it's simply too small. Most people want three or more bedrooms.

Therefore, even though personally two bedrooms may fit you very well, when a big reason for buying is investment, you need to consider how difficult it will be to sell such a home later on. Will most buyers want your home? Or will they look elsewhere?

If you are unreasonably narrowing the pool of potential buyers, perhaps it makes more sense to pass on this house and look for a bigger home. Of course, that means not catering to your desires. But, when it's time to resell, it likely will mean a quicker sale and more money in your pocket.

Here's a list of what other people tend to look for when buying a house. Most of these are probably your reasons as well. But not necessarily all.

Other People's House List

- Upscale location
- Newer home or at least upgraded and updated
- Good condition
- 3 or more bedrooms
- 2 or more baths
- At least a 2-car garage
- Maintenance-free yard

Buying to Get More Room

The reason many people buy a home is to move up in size. It could be because of an expanding family. Or it could be that their income has increased. Or it could simply be that they want a bigger (and often fancier) place to spread around in.

This translates into a house with more square footage and usually more bedrooms. If this is you, here are some things to consider:

- Most newer homes that are bigger are on postage stamp lots, hence to get more space they are on two levels. The second floor is usually as big as the first. And typically the bedrooms are upstairs and the living area downstairs. While that may make a kind of intuitive sense, if you have children do you want to be running up and down stairs with them all day? What about kids falling down stairs? If you're older, or ill, how easy will it be for you to get up and down those stairs?
- Today, most of the value of property is in the lot, not the house. When you pay more for a bigger house that's on a

smaller lot, it may not be a wise investment. It might be better to look for a bigger lot with a bigger single-story house.

- Will the bigger house fit you in the future? Statistically most people move about every eight to nine years. Will the bigger house do for the next eight to nine years? If your kids are teenagers, they may move out in four or five years, and then what will you do with a big house? If you're going to retire soon, will you want the financial burden of a bigger house?
- The bigger the home, the more costly it is to heat and cool. Are you prepared for the extra utility costs?

While your reason for buying may be to get a bigger home, you should carefully consider the consequences that greater size brings.

Buying to Get a Better Neighborhood

Usually people whose reason to buy is to get a better neighborhood really are moving in order to get away from a bad neighborhood. There's nothing wrong with this. However, you want to be careful that you don't jump from the frying pan into the fire. Be very careful when sizing up a new neighborhood. Here are some tips I use:

- **Check for graffiti.** Today it's common almost everywhere. But there's much less of it in better neighborhoods and what occurs there usually is washed or painted over immediately by homeowners who take pride in their homes. Remember, lots of graffiti usually means gangs and increased crime—just the sort of thing you may be moving away from.
- **Check for density.** The narrower the streets and the more crowded the housing, generally the noisier and more dissatisfying the living experience.

- **Check for past price appreciation.** An agent can usually give you a history of prices in a neighborhood going back over the last decade. Have prices kept up with national and state averages? Exceeded them? Fallen short? Generally a neighborhood that did well in the past should do well in the future.

- **Check with neighbors.** If you're going to buy a house, don't be hesitant to first knock on the door of your potential neighbors. After all, once you buy, it's too late—you can't move your neighbors away. Tell them you're planning to buy next door and want to know something about the neighborhood. Ask them about barking dogs and vandalism. Are they people you think you can get along with? Do they have children and pets? Are they well-behaved? What do their homes and lots look like—clean and neat, or a mess?

TRAP

A bad mistake is to leap first, only to discover later that what appeared to be a great neighborhood has serious problems.

Buying to Get Better Schools

In most locales, the public school your children attend is determined by where you live. Thus, the reason many people move is to get a home in a good school district.

If buying in a school district is important to you, it should be your first question to an agent. How good are the schools? How do you know?

Then, go to the schools and ask to see their test scores. Nearly all have national and/or state test scores that they will make available to you. Anything in the 90th or higher percentile is great. Anything below the 50th percentile is usually a red flag.

Also ask if the local school is a school of distinction, has won awards. Ask about the sports program and other extracurricular activities. The more the principal or school spokesperson brags about the school, the better.

TIP

The price of homes is directly linked to the quality of schools. The better the school district, the more expensive the homes . . . and vice versa. Yes, you'll pay more when you buy to get into a better school district. But you should be able to get more when you later resell.

Other considerations are how close is the home to the school? Can your children walk there? Is busing available, or will you have to drive them every day?

Also, find out how new the schools are. Today, public school districts everywhere are strapped for money and often don't have the funds to fix up or even maintain older buildings.

Buying to Get Closer to Work

Congestion is the bane of our modern American society. Fifty years ago, even 15 years ago, it was common for workers to live great distances from their homes and commute. This is especially the case where there are freeways, thruways, or toll roads. For example, in California, where I hail from, it was nothing for a person to live in Stockton and commute daily to San Jose—a distance of about 70 miles. It would take about an hour and a half.

Today, however, such a commute might be considered suicidal because of the traffic, road delays, and cost of fuel. Although with off-hour traffic the trip might still take an hour and a half, in rush-hour traffic it could take three hours or longer, in each direction.

TRAP

Today it's not how far away from work you live. It's how long it takes you to get there.

Homes in Stockton tend to be less expensive than those in San Jose—hence the motive for the long commute.

Nevertheless, many people are opting to pay more to live closer. Many feel life is too short and precious to be wasted in a car stuck in traffic.

If you're buying to get closer, here are some tips to consider:

- **It's time, not distance.** Is the new house truly closer than the old? Sometimes a shorter distance takes a longer time. *During rush hour*, before you buy, drive the route between the home and your work. Check not how far it is in miles, but how long it really takes. You may be surprised . . . and decide to look in a different direction.

- **Get closer.** Consider older neighborhoods closer to the central city. While many were run down and left to deteriorate in the past, today these almost blighted areas are coming back in force as people like yourself look for locations closer to the city center. Catch a neighborhood as it's being revitalized and you could buy in for a song and get a home much closer to work.

- **Remember that jobs change.** It would be a shame to buy closer to work, only to be transferred or lose your job. Consider your job's stability realistically before buying.

TIP

Sometimes it is easier and less costly to get a new job than to get a new house!

Buying to Get a More Energy-Efficient House

In case you hadn't noticed, the price of utilities has been skyrocketing. Natural gas, propane, fuel oil all have doubled, tripled, and, in some cases, quadrupled. In areas of severe climate (snow in winter, heat in summer) it's not uncommon to see heating or cooling bills of $500 a month or more for an average-sized home.

Today, water costs more; garbage service, more; electricity for lighting, more. I don't recall seeing any area of the country where the prices have gone down . . . or even stabilized. Everything costs more by huge amounts.

Thus, while it's rarely the first reason given for buying a home, getting a house that's more energy efficient, hence less costly to run, is typically one of the reasons for buying that people give.

If this is a consideration for you, then here are tips to consider:

- **Is the home newer?** Newer homes tend to have more insulation, tighter-fitting and more energy-conserving windows and doors, and they usually are built with energy efficiency in mind. For example, you may not have noticed, but, in general, modern homes have less window area than older homes. The reason is that windows allow an easier transmission of heat than walls and some doors. Hence, the fewer windows, the "tighter" the house. Homes more than 50 years old tend to be real energy losers, unless they have been updated.

- **Does it have double-pane windows?** You can cut your energy bills by more than 10 percent simply by having double-pane windows. If you're considering an older home with single-pane windows, keep in mind that it will cost close to $10,000 to replace the old single panes with double panes.

- **Is the home insulated?** Homes built before about 1975 seldom had much insulation. A home without insulation can have an enormous amount of heat transfer, as much as 50 percent more than an insulated home.

TRAP

Beware of buying an uninsulated home with the intention of insulating it. While blowing insulation into an attic is inexpensive and very effective, it is almost impossible to retrofit insulation into walls. When it is done, it tends to be extremely expensive and not always effective.

- **Are the heating and cooling systems newer?** In the last few years, the efficiency of heating and cooling systems has increased enormously. Even a heater or air conditioner that's just 10 years old may only be 60 or 70 percent as efficient as a newer model. Check for the SAR on air conditioners and the efficiency rating on furnaces. (Look for at least 13 SAR and an efficiency of 90 percent or better on furnaces.) Keep in mind that replacing both heating and air-conditioning, including new insulated ducts, can easily cost $10,000 or more.
- **Is the house "green"?** Green homes tend to recycle waste, have latent heating and cooling systems, and often have wonderful garden areas. Be careful, however. Not all things that are green are inexpensive.

Is It a Good Fit?

Finally, the reason you buy a home should be because it fits you and your family well. There are many factors to consider. Here are some tips I like.

Checking for Fit

YOU'VE GOT	YOU NEED
Working spouses	One (or two) home office(s)
Two who cook	Big kitchen
Stuff to store	3-car garage
Entertain a lot	A "great room"
Stay at home	TV/entertainment room
Two separate adults	Two master bedroom suites
Small children	Lots of bedrooms/laundry
Older children	Sound-insulated rooms
Sports oriented	Near recreation center/pool
Handyman	3-car garage
Relaxation lover	Spa/sauna
Pet(s)	Large fenced yard
Snow country	Mud/exercise room

What You Can and Cannot Afford

f I were writing this chapter before the mortgage meltdown of 2007 and 2008, it simply would be one sentence long: Go see a mortgage broker and get preapproved. That's all there was to it back then. The lender would look at your preapproval and tell you how big a mortgage you could afford—what the payments and the minimum down payment would be and that was that. You could bank on it.

Today, it's a different story.

Many premeltdown lenders abused the process. Based on preapprovals, some lenders assured borrowers that they could afford to buy much more expensive homes with bigger mortgages than they could truly afford. They encouraged borrowers to "stretch" and obtain sophisticated mortgages that, apparently, many of them did not fully understand.

These special mortgages were usually ARMs (adjustable-rate mortgages) that offered astoundingly low initial monthly payments. They accomplished this by having very low interest rates, at least at first. Called "teasers," these low initial interest rates (sometimes as low as 3 percent or less!) cut payments from what they should have been at true market interest rates by a third, sometimes more. In other words, if the mortgage should have a monthly payment of $1,000, these teasers brought it down as low as $600, sometimes less!

The problem was twofold. First the lenders would look at the buyers' preapproval, and if it said they could afford $600 a month (in our example), they'd approve the buyers for the loan. No, they probably couldn't afford the higher $1,000 monthly payment, but if they could afford the low teaser, they got the mortgage.

What's wrong with that?

Nothing, if the mortgage payment remained constant for the life of the loan. The problem was that it didn't. It typically reset to the much higher market rate after two years. Two years into ownership, the borrowers discovered that their payments almost doubled! Of course, most simply couldn't afford to pay that much. (Their preapproval usually said just that.) Abruptly the borrowers learned that they really couldn't afford that house they had bought with the fancy mortgage.

Enter Mortgage Plan "B"

So they did what the lenders had assured them they would be able to do when the mortgage reset, the payments rose, and they couldn't afford them. They attempted to refinance to another mortgage with another low teaser rate and correspondingly low payments. They tried to do it all over again.

However, times had changed. It was 2007 and 2008 and there was an enormous credit crunch. Most of those teaser mortgages were no longer available. Further, requirements for new loans were stricter. The mortgages that their lenders had assured them would be available simply weren't there. That meant that the poor borrowers now couldn't refinance out of the onerous mortgages they had obtained.

So borrowers were faced with a monthly payment that was unaffordable. And being unable to refinance, most borrowers tried to sell.

Only it was the end of the "bubble." House values dropped and that meant that very often the lower value of the house was less than the mortgage. Their equity was gone. And they couldn't "give the property away." They were "upside down." Now, not only couldn't they refinance; they couldn't resell.

The result was the biggest number of foreclosures in modern times. (There probably were more foreclosures during the Great Depression of the 1930s, but accurate records are not available.) Millions of borrowers were faced with losing their property.

The moral of that sad story is you don't want to be like them. Unless you want to risk foreclosure yourself, before buying you're going to have to do some work to determine what you can afford. And what you cannot afford. That's what this chapter will help you do.

Should You Get Preapproved?

From the previous discussion, you might think I was knocking preapproval. I'm not. Only today I suggest you use it as only one tool to help you get a mortgage. The other tools should be your common sense and some rather pointed questions you need to ask a lender. (And be sure to get their answers in writing—lenders won't honor anything you tell them unless it's written down and signed—you should return the favor.)

Preapproval takes perhaps half an hour or so of your time. Just contact a local lender or mortgage broker or, what's even easier, go online. There are hundreds of mortgage brokers that can easily help you get preapproved. Check out www.eloan.com, www.quickenloan.com, and www.lendingtree.com.

You'll be asked to fill out an application, provide some documentation, and that's it. It might cost you $35 for a credit report (or it might not depending on how good your lender/mortgage broker is), but that's really a very small investment. You'll have your answer in a few days or less. It will tell you, basically, how big a monthly payment you can afford. From that information it's easy to derive how big a mortgage you can get.

Now Comes the Tricky Part

Preapproval doesn't tell you what type of loan you can qualify for. That's the lender's job. When you go to a lender, it's up to you to ask about a mortgage—what its pros and cons are. Here are some very important questions you should ask the lender.

Questions You Should Ask Your Lender before Getting a Mortgage

- Will my monthly payments remain constant for the life of the mortgage (a fixed-rate loan)?
- Can my monthly payment change during the course of the loan (an ARM)?
- If adjustable, how long before the *first* adjustment or the reset of my monthly payments? (How long is the teaser good for?)
- If the mortgage were to reset today, based on current interest rates, what would my new payment be? (Ask yourself, "If I can't afford the new bigger payment today, will I be able to afford it tomorrow?")

- Based on interest rate performance over the past 25 years, what is the likelihood that my payment will reset higher? Lower?

Keep your eye on interest rates. No matter what type of mortgage you get, the higher the market interest rate, the higher your monthly payments and, correspondingly, the smaller the mortgage you will qualify for.

What About the Down Payment?

Thus far, we've only been discussing the mortgage amount. But what about the down payment? How big a down payment will I be required to make?

Again, the answer will come from your preapproval and will reflect your credit standing and income. The better your credit and income, the lower the down payment you'll need. The lower your credit and income, the higher a down payment you'll need.

Your preapproval letter generally will indicate the minimum down payment you will need to make. Of course, there's nothing to say that you can't put down more.

For those with low incomes and sometimes not quite perfect credit, there are special loans. These are offered by the FHA (a federal agency that insures mortgages) and Freddie Mac and Fannie Mae (quasi government agencies that buy mortgages on the secondary market from the lender you deal directly with—the primary market). These mortgages typically offer lower down payments, sometimes nothing down, and may even help with the closing costs! Ask your mortgage broker about them.

Today, most borrowers are looking at a minimum of 10 percent down. Some 5 percent and a very few zero percent mortgages are still available, but they are far rarer than in the past. Twenty percent down, the standard of years ago, is making a big revival.

Don't Forget Closing Costs

When you're told the minimum down payment you'll be required to make, don't think you're home free. There will also be closing costs. These can add thousands more to the deal.

Closing costs pay for such things as:

- Escrow
- Title insurance
- Tax pro rations
- Mortgage points and fees

The lender is required to give you a RESPA form (mailed to you within three days of giving you a mortgage application), which is an estimate of your closing costs. Unfortunately, lenders are notorious for not sticking to those estimates.

A good real estate agent can often give you a better estimate of your true costs, sometimes to within $50!

Why *Do* People Opt for the ARM with a Teaser?

This is the insidious part. Often you can get a far bigger mortgage with an ARM-teaser than with a fixed rate. The reason, of course, is that the ARM-teaser has a much lower initial interest rate, which translates into lower payments.

Thus, for any given maximum payment, the ARM-teaser mortgage is almost always higher than the fixed-rate mortgage. And getting a bigger mortgage can mean the difference between being able to buy that wonderfully big house in a great neighborhood you've always wanted, or having to settle for a much smaller property in a lesser part of town.

We've discussed some of the traps with an ARM-teaser: when the mortgage resets (adjusts upward) you may not be able to make the payments, may not be able to refinance, and may not be able to sell. On the surface it's a no-brainer. Why would anyone go for the ARM-teaser?

But, underneath there's the burning desire to get that better house in that better area. Thus, many borrowers throw caution to the winds. They bet that within two years or so when the ARM-teaser resets, they'll figure something out. Maybe their income will have increased to the point where they can afford those higher payments. Maybe the market will have turned around and they can resell at a profit. Maybe the refi market will be looser.

Of course, any of those things may happen. Or not.

It's Your Decision

Nobody will decide for you to get one kind of a mortgage or another. It really comes down to how conservative you are in your finances.

But, if you decide to take a fling with an ARM-teaser and things don't work out, don't come back crying later. You've been forewarned!

Make sure you get a committed preapproval letter.

Today virtually all lenders will take a look at your credit history, your income, and your assets and then, based on underwriting standards, issue you a preapproval letter. If they've actually gotten a credit report on you, checked with your employer, and looked at your bank statements, this is a preapproval commitment that you can "take to the bank."

TRAP

Beware of being simply "qualified."

On the other hand, a mortgage broker or even a real estate agent can ask you a couple of financial questions over the phone and then send you a preapproval letter. However, if your credit report wasn't checked, if your income and assets weren't verified, if underwriting standards weren't applied (and if it wasn't issued directly by a reputable lender), it probably isn't worth the paper it's written on. The reason is simple: no lender will back it up.

What Does Your Budget Say?

Okay, *now* it's time to take a reality check. A realistic look at your budget can give you a good idea of what you will feel comfortable about spending on a mortgage.

It's not hard. Just calculate your total spendable monthly income. That's what you get after taxes, alimony, and other amounts are taken out.

Then subtract what the preapproval letter says you can afford monthly and see what's left. Can you really live on that for a month?

TIP

Don't forget to factor in tax and interest deductions.

Remember, you can deduct the interest on your mortgage (up to very high limits) and your property taxes from your ordinary income. By adjusting your W-4 form with your employer, you can factor this in and get a higher monthly take-home paycheck. Be sure to ask your accountant.

Your Reality Check 1

Take-home pay (after increasing for mortgage
interest and property tax deductions) $_____
Monthly payment (including taxes and insurance)
as determined by the lender $_____
What's left for you? $_____

Budgeting to Determine How Big a Payment You Can Afford

Income

$_____	Net*
$_____	Increase after calculation for interest and property tax deductions
$_____	Increase after eliminating voluntary deductions

Less Expenses

$_____	Utilities (Gas, electric, water, garbage)
$_____	Phone
$_____	Cable/Satellite TV
$_____	Auto (Lease/Purchase payment, insurance, gas)
$_____	Food
$_____	Entertainment
$_____	Clothing
$_____	Child care
$_____	Tuition (private schools)
$_____	Maintenance (gardening, painting, etc.)
$_____	Repairs
$_____	Child support/Alimony
$_____	Medical (services, drugs)
$_____	Recreation (gym, sports, etc.)
$_____	Unpaid credit card debt†
$_____	Long-term loans
$_____	Total Expenses
$_____	Income Available for Mortgage Payment

*It's important to remember that your net monthly income is after voluntary deductions such as 401(k) contributions, which can be reduced or eliminated. Also remember, some of your involuntary deductions, such as for taxes, should be reduced because of the deduction you'll get for home mortgage interest and taxes, thus increasing your take-home pay. (See Chapter 2.)

†Unpaid credit card debt is the worst type of liability because it's paid back at extraordinarily high interest rates. Try to pay this down or refinance it into long-term debt before moving to make a home purchase. Lots of credit card debt may cause lenders to reject you for a mortgage.

Few people want to radically change their lifestyles in order to buy a home. So be realistic with the numbers.

Take a few minutes to determine what your true monthly living expenses are. (Don't forget medicines, entertainment, eating out, and so on.) On the other hand, for a home that will give you privacy, security, and, in the long run, equity build-up, you might very well want to give up living in a princely style. What you need to decide is what you can live without and what you absolutely must have. Use the chart on the previous page to help you figure it out.

Add up all of those monthly items you *must have*. Now compare the total to "what's left for you" after making your house payment, as determined earlier.

Your Reality Check 2

What's left for me	$_____
What I must have to live on	$_____

If "What's left for me" is bigger, congratulations. The lender's computer was right and you can easily make those monthly payments!

If "What I must have to live on" is bigger, whoa! You'll either have to tighten your belt more, OR you'll have to reduce your monthly payment, cut back on the size of your mortgage, and purchase a smaller house. Otherwise, reconsider renting.

Picking the Right Agent

Most people think picking real estate agents is like picking apples out of a barrel. There are going to be a few shiny ones at the top, a few bad ones on the bottom, but overall they are going to be pretty much the same. Like apples, one agent is pretty much like another.

Unfortunately, that's not the case.

Yes, the vast majority of agents are honest and endeavor to do a good job for you, their clients. The real distinction, however, is not so much to do with ethics as with ability. Some agents are truly able to help you. Unfortunately, many are not.

It's important to understand what I mean by "ability." I'm not talking about understanding the laws of your state with regard to the licensing of agents or the selling of real estate. Today, in all states agents must pass strict tests as well as continue their education to make sure they understand what their legal and fiduciary responsibilities are. In this sense, the overwhelming number of agents are capable. It's when it comes to finding the right property and negotiating the best deal for you that many fall down.

My father, who was a successful agent for over 30 years, used to say, "When I first got my license, I thought I was ready to sell real estate. It wasn't until 10 years later that I finally learned how to really be an agent." To understand what he meant, it's important to realize just what's involved in being a real estate agent. Once you see the selling of property from the agent's perspective, you may get a whole new view of how to pick the right one.

What's Involved in Being a Good Real Estate Agent?

According to the Hollywood stereotype, the typical real estate agent drives a big Mercedes or a Caddy, Lexus, or BMW. He or she (most agents are women) meets clients over cocktails, attends flashy parties with lenders, and makes oodles of money (often into seven figures, but certainly into six figures).

The truth is somewhat less exciting. According to several surveys, a successful agent with at least 10 years' experience in 2007 took home under $60,000 a year. In other words, the typical real estate agent was not a high roller, but a pretty modest earner in terms of income from real estate.

"How can that be?" I'm sure you're asking. The commissions are big and chances are the agents you've met always seemed so successful.

The truth? Often it's mostly a front. A lot of agents simply work hard at looking successful.

Part-Timers

You also have to understand that real estate is actually a second or part-time career for many individuals. It attracts a large number of people who are looking for less than full-time work. Typically these are people who have retired from another career (teaching, the military, government, or large corporations are typical) and are now on a pension and/or Social Security and are looking to pick up a few extra bucks.

Often these people have dabbled a little in real estate themselves and are in an office as much to look for bargains they can buy on their own as to service you. In the trade these people are sometimes called "inactive" agents.

I have nothing against part-time or inactive agents. Some provide excellent service to you, their clients. In fact, at some point in your life you may want to dabble in real estate and may become one yourself! It's a great way to get a little extra income on the side.

The difficulty I have with many inactive agents who have another steady source of income is that they may not be "hungry" enough to get out there, find the really good houses, and negotiate the toughest deals. (After all, whether they make a sale or not they know they'll survive—because of their other income.)

How many "inactive" agents are out there? A lot. Try to remember the 80/20 rule-of-thumb. Every active real estate broker (and I was one for many years) knows that 20 percent of the agents sell 80 percent of the property. The corollary is that 80 percent of the agents are only selling 20 percent of the property. That big 80 percent includes many of the "inactive" group.

You Want the Hot 20 Percent

Let's talk about that 20 percent that's making the vast majority of deals. These typically are the "active" agents. They tend to be aggressive, often relatively young individuals who have no means of support other than real estate. To put it bluntly, if they don't make deals, they don't eat.

If you were to isolate this group of individuals, you would find that each typically makes around $100,000 a year and probably half make substantially more. They are out there beating the bushes from dawn till dusk. They look at *every* new house that comes on the market in their area. They are constantly "farming" (talking with potential sellers) to get listings. In today's market, they are the ones who know where the good foreclosures are, often before they are made public. When they get an offer, they go in there and negotiate all night if necessary to get the best deal for you.

Is this the agent you want working for you? You bet it is!

The Three Most Important Questions to Ask Your Agent

1. **How long have you been full-time?** Avoid part-time agents, or those with fewer than five years of active experience.

2. **What neighborhoods (or area) do you "farm"?** "Farming" is where agents go door-to-door soliciting listings—they intimately learn the neighborhood, learn when properties are coming up for sale, and can tell you off the top of their heads what's available right now. Ideally the agent's farm is where you want to buy.

3. **How much time and effort will you commit to me?** You want someone who will be ready to go whenever you are, phones you regularly with updates, and continually previews properties for you.

How Do You Separate the Active from the Inactive Agents?

You want an active agent. How do you get one? First off, remember that active agents are *active*. They spend most of their time working on real estate.

Identifying the Active Agent

- Has lots of listings.
- Works tirelessly at real estate, including evenings and weekends.
- Is extremely familiar with the market in your area.
- Is ready and able to give you references of numerous buyers from sales made *in the past few months.*
- Is busy, but not too busy for you.
- Is experienced and "up to speed" with at least five years actively in the business.

TIP

A recommendation from a friend always is a good method of finding the active agent. If your friend has had a positive experience with an agent, it's a good sign. But remember, it's not a guarantee. Your friend might have just been lucky and fallen into the perfect house—the agent's efforts could have been incidental. Even with a recommendation, you need to check to be sure you've got an active agent.

Are There Active versus Inactive Offices?

Just as there are active/inactive agents, there are also active/inactive offices. The active offices are where sales are constantly happening. The inactive offices are where the agents sit around and commiserate with one another about the slow (to them) real estate market.

Here are good ways to tell the two types of offices apart:

How to Identify Active from Inactive Offices

- An active office almost always advertises heavily. Check the ads in your local paper.
- An active office usually has quite a few agents, and they always seem to be scurrying around or out in the field,

not sitting at their desks drinking coffee and reading the newspaper.

- An active office usually has promotions going on to induce greater activity from agents. Walking in, you will often see "salesperson of the month" and "lister of the month" awards, which might be TVs or trips to Hawaii for the best producers of the season, and so on.

- Other agents will know of the active offices and often will speak of them grudgingly as people who are always getting the deals done.

- This is just a personal observation, but I have found that active offices usually have a secretarial staff. The agents are out there selling, the staff handles the paperwork. In an inactive office (without many sales or much revenue), it seems the agents are stuck with all the secretarial duties.

Just keep in mind that the 80/20 rule still applies, even in an active office. It's just that in an inactive office, the hot 20 percent aren't there at all.

How Do You Find an Active Agent in an Active Office?

If you walk off the street into an active real estate office, chances are actually against your getting an active agent. The reason is that all agents pull "floor time." This is time they are expected to sit in the office and pick up potential clients who come in across the transom.

You walk in and you get the current floor agent or, if there's a receptionist, the next agent who is "up." You'll immediately know this person. How? While other people in the office smile at you, this agent will quickly come up, introduce herself or himself, and ask how she or he can be helpful.

Since almost all agents, active or inactive, are people-oriented, they almost certainly will be polite, charming, and apparently help-ful. But if they are inactive agents, they could be wasting your time.

Don't get the agent who's "up." When you walk into a real estate office cold, don't accept the first agent who comes to see you. Rather, say that you are waiting to see someone, an agent, but you can't remember the name. Now, while the receptionist or the floor agent begins listing the names of the agents in the company, look around the walls of the reception area. As noted, a great many active companies will have "agent of the month" awards hanging there. Very frequently, the award for the past 10 or 12 months will have gone repeatedly to one agent. Just point to the plaque and say, "That's her," or "That's him." You'll be quickly introduced to the most active agent in the office. If there are no awards to tip you off, then ask to see the broker.

It's important to understand that most real estate offices are organized around one person, the broker. Everyone else is an associate agent. (Even other brokers may have their licenses subordinated to the main broker.)

In a small office, the broker acts as a salesperson. In a larger office, however, the broker typically sits somewhere in a back office and handles closings and other difficult work. In a very large office, the broker frequently may be out making big deals while subordinate brokers handle the day-to-day work.

When you request the broker by name, you are usually asked in response, "Will your name be recognized by our broker?" In other words, do you have an appointment?

Just reply, "My business concerns one of your agents. I want to speak only to the broker." Just the hint that there could be some problem will get you an audience. Real estate companies dread complaints or angry clients. Most will bend over backward to avoid any kind of dissatisfaction.

When you are ushered in to see the broker (or the person who is in charge at the moment in the case of a very large office), carefully explain that you have not yet talked to any agent in the office (thereby avoiding the problem of having one agent or another "claim" you as a client). Tell the broker you are going to be buying a house in the very near future and you want to deal with the most active agent in the office in terms of sales. No one else will do.

The broker may chuckle inwardly at your boldness, but in most cases will tell you who that agent is. And you're on your way. (If the broker refuses, leave. There are almost as many real estate companies to choose from as there are houses for sale!)

Should You Aim for a Large "Franchise" Real Estate Company?

Don't be misled into picking your agent on the basis of the real estate company's name recognition. Over the past few decades, franchising has proliferated in the real estate market. But a real estate franchise is no better or worse than a fast-food franchise such as McDonald's or Burger King. All that you are assured of in a fast-food franchise is that you will get no less than a certain quality standard of hamburger and service. Most people will agree that you're not guaranteed to get the tastiest burger in town. The same holds true for real estate franchises.

In most cases, each real estate office, regardless of the franchise name, is individually owned and operated. What you're dealing with is the local broker and agents who have adopted the sign, the sports coat, and the procedures of a franchising company. However, you still go out with your individual agent to see properties, and it's your agent with whom you'll consult when making an offer.

The franchise office may be no better or worse than a nonfranchised office in providing you with good, active agents—it does, however, have name recognition, policies and procedures, more advertising clout, and sometimes nicer jackets.

When comparing top agents, I don't feel there's a significant difference between companies. (Some franchises offer their own financing and escrows, which can be a convenience. But in my opinion, it's always better to get your own financing and use an independent escrow, anyhow.)

Go with the agent, not the company.

On the other hand, if something should go wrong, sometimes it's easier (sometimes harder!) to deal with a franchise company. At least you know it's a big corporate entity that is concerned with keeping its good name and its customers happy. And it probably has deep pockets.

It's important to remember that real estate, almost more than any other business, is highly personalized. The deal you get will depend mostly on the one person with whom you deal. You can get a great active agent with a nonfranchised company just as well as with a franchised one.

How Do You Help an Agent Help You?

Once you find a good active agent, you must decide whether he or she is right for you. Watch for obvious problems such as personality clashes or basic differences in outlook.

Agents can influence your decisions by what they do or do not say. Be sure that they aren't using this power to manipulate you into something you may not want. You want to be sure that the agent isn't so aggressive as to overwhelm you. You want to be able to control your agent, not the other way around.

You will want to be forthright with an agent. Let the agent know your price range. Tell the agent the areas you want to locate to. Show the agent your preapproval letter. (If you're not sure what that is, reread the last chapter.)

The agent isn't a mind reader and can't find the perfect house for you unless and until you give the agent the parameters of what you're looking for. This doesn't mean you need to tell agents everything about your finances or your intentions, as we'll see shortly. Just offer enough to enable them to work for you.

Should You Work with Several Agents?

The best rule to follow is to work with only one agent at a time. Don't hip-hop from one to the next. Only when your relationship peters out and the agent stops showing you properties should you want to move on.

TIP

Reward a good agent with your loyalty, and the agent will reward you with good work.

As noted, only when you find that your current agent is no longer productive, should you try another. But be "up front" with both agents. Tell the second agent the properties you've already seen. Ask the second agent for something new or different to show you. Tell the first agent you're leaving . . . and why.

Is Working with More Than One Agent over Time Better?

Sometimes.

While the vast majority of properties listed by agents are put on the Multiple Listing Service (MLS), where nearly all agents can work on them, some agents keep really good properties to themselves, sometimes called "vest pocket listings." As a result, other agents simply don't know about them and, therefore, can't show you the properties. Further, in some areas, realty companies won't put any or all of their listings on the MLS. As a result, any one agent may not be able to show you all the properties that are listed.

On the other hand, understand that the agent who first shows you the property you eventually buy may be entitled to a portion of the commission even if a different agent eventually makes the sale. This could cause hard feelings or even problems later on should a different agent submit the offer. Instead of working hard to negotiate the best price and terms for you, the various agents could get into a squabble over who gets what portion of the commission.

Work with only one agent at a time and tell that agent the properties you've already seen and whom else you've worked with. It will save you time and possible problems later on.

TRAP

Beware the overly aggressive agent. Years ago (before the consumer protection movement was even dreamed of) I knew an agent who had a very aggressive style. He would get his clients in his car, which was connected to his office by two-way radio. (This was before cellular phones.) He would then take them out looking at properties. After he had exhausted his immediate list of properties, he would call his office and ask his secretary to look up other properties to show. Some clients were impressed. They would continue to look until they were exhausted and then ask to be taken back to the office, where their car was parked. The agent would refuse! Oh, he wouldn't exactly say, "No!" Instead, he'd tell them about some other house that was just around the corner and was just right for them. He literally kept them prisoner in his car until they finally agreed to make an offer! Of course, they could always have made him stop and then gotten out. But more often than not, the clients were new to the area and had no idea where they were. While some clients did get angry and refuse to consider anything until the agent brought them back, a surprising number actually were coerced into making offers!

Fortunately, such actions today are unheard of. But the story illustrates an important point. Some agents are more actively aggressive than you want or can handle. If that's the case, run, don't walk, away. They'll try to coerce you into bad deals every time.

The Agent's Loyalty Is Not Always to You!

This is a most important point that most buyers simply don't understand. Let's say that you've found an active agent whom you like and with whom you can work. You must now come to grips with the fact that, in many cases, this agent *does not work for you!* He or she may be the agent of, and work for, the seller.

It doesn't matter that your agent shows you around to many houses listed by other agents on the Multiple Listing Service. It doesn't matter that the house you decide to make an offer on has a separate agent who listed it. (This can be confusing to buyers, particularly when very often there is one agent—yours—who shows you a house and takes your offer and another agent—the one who listed the property—who seems to represent the seller. Actually, the agent who shows you around may be the "subagent" of the agent who listed the property. In other words, *both* may be the agents of the seller!)

The person to whom an agent is responsible is called his or her fiduciary relationship. And it turns out that depends on whom the agent declares for. It could be for you. But it might be for the seller.

TIP

Find out your agent's fiduciary relationship. An agent *must declare* whom he or she represents. Who pays the agent, who goes out with the agent, whom the agent talks to doesn't matter. It's whom the agent declares for that counts.

What does having a fiduciary relationship mean? It means that the agent owes the seller "integrity, honesty, and loyalty." That translates into the following.

The Effects of Dealing with a Seller's Agent

Unless the seller has authorized it, in theory your seller's agent can't disclose to you how much less than the selling price the seller might take, even if the agent knows of a specific figure. That would be disloyal to the seller. (This isn't to say that many seller's agents don't hint at the lower figure, but they aren't supposed to come right out and tell you, for example, that the seller said, "My price is $100,000, but I'm so desperate to sell I'd take $75,000, *but don't you dare tell that to any buyer!*")

The seller's agent can't disclose that the seller might accept terms more favorable to you unless the seller has authorized the agent to tell you.

On the other hand, if you tell the seller's agent that you're desperate to buy, that even though you're offering $175,000 you'd be willing to pay $200,000, the agent is *obligated* to tell the seller what you said!

TRAP

Working with a seller's agent is almost like having an enemy spy in your camp! Of course, in actual practice there is some bending of the rules. And a good agent will always attempt to work fairly with both buyer and seller.

In today's world, where consumers are so litigious, many sellers' agents are hesitant to do anything that sellers might construe as violating the fiduciary relationship and become angry over it (read as threaten a lawsuit). Hence, when you work with a seller's agent (or subagent), don't expect advice on how to get the best terms or price.

TIP

When you're working with a seller's agent, even one you consider to be on your side, button your lips. Don't tell the seller's agent the highest you'll go on an offer. Remember the old World War II slogan about "loose lips sink ships." Don't let the agent know the best terms you'll give the seller. Think of the agent as the seller's earphone. Don't whisper anything that you don't want the seller to hear. Keep your own confidences.

What About a Buyer's Agent?

One answer for buyers is the buyer's agent. A buyer's agent declares for the buyer and works for you.

That doesn't necessarily mean that you always have to pay the buyer's agent. Usually the buyer's agent and the seller's agent split the commission that the seller pays.

However, keep in mind that if the seller refuses to pay the buyer's agent, you might be asked to pay his or her share of the commission. That, of course, is usually negotiated *before* a deal is completed.

What About a Dual Agent?

A dual agent represents *both* buyer and seller. This agent owes both the seller and you, the buyer, "integrity, honesty, and loyalty." The way this sometimes works is that the dual agent may not tell you if the seller will accept a price less than the property is listed for. However, to compensate for this, the dual agent may also not tell the seller that you'd be willing to pay more than the price you offer. (The same generally holds true with terms.)

Thus, while the dual agent really isn't 100 percent on your side, the agent also isn't 100 percent on the seller's side either. The dual agent tries to walk a fine line working for both buyer and seller.

Dual Agent versus Buyer's Agent versus Seller's Agent

Dual Agency.   The agent represents both you and the seller and the agent tries to avoid telling either party anything that will hurt the other. Usually this means not saying anything that will benefit you at the expense of the seller.

Buyer's Agent.   The agent represents just you and must tell you if he or she learns something that will benefit you, even at the expense of the seller.

Seller's Agent.   The agent represents just the sellers and must tell them if he or she learns something to their benefit, even if it's at your expense.

How Do You Know Whom Your Agent Is Working For?

Ask.

Your agent is obligated to tell you. Further, before you sign any documents to a deal, including a sales offer, your agent should present you with a written statement describing whom that agent works for (seller, dual, or buyer). Many states now require a formal disclosure as part of their agency law.

TRAP

Don't assume that just because your agent isn't the lister of the property she automatically is your (buyer's) agent. She might be the seller's or a "dual" agent. Ask your agent to declare her loyalty.

Should You Work with a "Buyer's Agent"?

There are some good reasons for you to work with a buyer's agent. After all, it's the only way you can be sure the agent is fully on your side. Remember, a true buyer's agent has a fiduciary responsibility to you, not to the seller. Such agents must tell you everything they know about the property and about the seller that's to your advantage, including any information about the seller's willingness to accept a lower price or better terms.

The only potential problem in dealing with a buyer's agent usually is the fee. As noted earlier, if you want a buyer's agent, and if the seller's agent refuses to split, you might have to pay the commission yourself.

Commissions

Here are the facts on real estate commissions:

- All commissions are negotiable, although the average today is 4 to 6 percent.
- With most properties there's a buyer's commission and a seller's and typically it's split down the middle.
- The seller usually pays the full commission including your buyer's agent half of the commission.
- The commission is usually paid to the seller's broker, who splits it with the buyer's broker, who then splits it with the salesperson, who is probably the person working with you. The split varies. The better the salesperson, typically the higher the split.

TRAP

Some brokers try to impose an additional "transaction fee"—this is in addition to the regular commission. They claim they need it in order to recover some of their costs. Many buyers refuse to pay.

Thus, having a buyer's agent may cost you no more than if you had worked with a seller's or a dual agent. On the other hand, by working with a buyer's agent, you might save so much on the purchase price that it would be worth your while to pay a commission yourself!

What About the "Bad Apples"?

As noted earlier, in every profession there are always a few bad apples. (Remember, the vast majority of agents are hard-working people who strive to do a good job.) In real estate these bad apples are agents who either are outright crooks or are so unaware of real estate laws that they can cause you harm in a deal. How do you avoid these?

Fortunately, in most cases the bad apples don't last long. After a few deals they often mess up so badly that there are letters of complaint to the state real estate regulatory body, which either revokes their licenses or disciplines them. The danger is that you might run into one of these bad apples before he or she gets thrown out. How do you protect yourself?

I wish I had a surefire answer. However, the tips here are the same ones that are given when picking any person to whom you give your confidence when it comes to your finances:

Avoiding the Bad Apples

- **Find out how long the agent has been in the business.** Even if the salesperson has been in business only a few years, the office should have been around a long time. Try to do business only with an agent or office that has a long track record—five years at the least.
- **Work with a national franchisee.** While earlier I stressed that this is no guarantee you'll get an active agent, it does give you some assurance of at least minimal quality in terms of procedures. Besides, if the agent should be truly incompetent and negligent, you can always appeal to the national office of the chain.
- **Ask to see the agent's real estate license.** In all states, agents *must be licensed* and that license must be prominently displayed in their office. They'll be pleased to show it to you.
- **Ask if the agent is a Realtor.** This is a member of the National Association of Realtors (NAR), which helps educate agents and promotes better business practices.

- **Ask for recommendations.** Call people the agent has dealt with in the past. See what they say. Ask if they would deal with this agent again.
- **Check with the local better business bureau** or (in an extreme case) the local district attorney's office to see if there are now pending or have ever been any complaints against the agent or the office.
- **Call the state real estate department** and ask if the agent's license has ever been revoked or suspended or if the agent has ever been disciplined. (This is public information to which you are entitled.)

Quite frankly, few buyers will ever take these last two steps. In most cases, we tend to accept a friendly smile and a solid handshake as evidence of competency and honesty. And in most cases things work out just fine. Remember, however, we are now considering those very few bad apples.

The worst thing that you can do is to find out you've been dealing with a bad agent after something has happened—after you've made an offer that has somehow gone awry and has resulted in a money loss to you or the threat of a lawsuit from the seller or some other injured party. A few calls may suddenly tell you that this agent has been in hot water since she got her license.

TIP

Many states have "Recovery Funds." If you have been damaged by an agent's actions, you may be able to recover at least a portion of the damages from the fund. Check with your state's department of real estate.

Then you'll say to yourself, "If only I had investigated first!" Remember, it takes only one or two phone calls and perhaps 15 minutes of time talking to the right people to get a minimal background check on the person who is going to advise you on what is probably the biggest investment you'll make in your life. No, it won't give you proof positive. But, it's a very good start.

Picking the right agent is one of the most important real estate decisions you'll ever make. Get it right the first time, and you'll have a friend and good financial advisor for many, many years.

Picking the Right Home

What's the right home for you?

Do you want three bedrooms? Four? More?

What about bathrooms? Can you live with one? What about three?

Many people prefer a newer home. The appliances are newer as are the features such as cabinets and countertops in kitchen and bathrooms. The layout is also often more pleasing. Do you want a newer home?

What about floors? Single story? Two/three story? Split level?

What about extra storage? An extra (three-car) garage? Special features such as a home office, fireplace, two master suites, pool/spa, and so on?

What about a big lot? A small one? A maintenance-free lot?

Is energy efficiency in the home important?

Do you want a single-family detached home? What about a zero-lot-line home (where one wall of the house is on the lot line and backs up to the neighbor)? What about a condo or co-op? What makes the right house for you?

What About Location?

Remember Chapter 2 where we talked about the most common reasons for buying? What do you want out of a location?

Is being close to work important to you?

Is an upscale neighborhood critical? What about an area that is in redevelopment?

Are good schools a priority?

What about proximity to shopping, recreation, medical facilities?

Are you especially concerned about crime and safety?

Use the following house-hunting checklist to help you determine just what it is you're looking for.

TIP

You won't get the home of your dreams until you first define just what that home is.

Narrowing Your Search

It's a matter of prioritizing.

Setting the parameters of your ideal house is important. There are so many houses out there today that without narrowing the

HOUSE-HUNTING CHECKLIST

House

- How many bedrooms do you need? _____
- How many bathrooms? _____
- Newer house? _____ Older home okay? _____
- Single-Story? _____ Two-Story? _____ Taller? _____
- Renovated kitchen and baths? _____
- Is storage important? _____
- Three-car garage? _____
- Place to park an RV? _____
- Room for a home office? _____
- Fireplace? _____
- Air-Conditioning? _____
- Pool/Spa? _____
- Big lot? _____ Small lot? _____ Maintenance-free lot? _____
- Two master suites? _____
- Willing to take a fixer-upper? _____

Location

- In a good school district? _____
- In an upscale neighborhood? _____
- In a low-crime neighborhood? _____
- Close to shopping? _____
- Close to work? _____
- Close to recreation? _____
- Close to medical facilities? _____

field, you could wander aimlessly amidst thousands of homes, never finding a satisfying property.

However, compromise is equally important. If you're like most buyers, it's unlikely you'll find just the home of your dreams, where you want it, at a price you can afford. Thus, you'll need to prioritize your search. You'll aim to get most of what you want, or at least the most important parts. But not necessarily all of what you want.

For example, if getting good schools is most important to you, you may need to settle for a smaller house and lot. If you must have a lot of bedrooms, you may need to get a home in a less upscale area. And so on.

As you begin searching homes out there, you'll very quickly get up to speed on what's available and what you can afford. Then it's a matter of applying your priorities.

Starting Your House-Hunting Search

Okay, let's say that you have an idea of what you want and you're ready to begin looking. Where do you start?

Today, most people start on the Internet. The most popular house-hunting site is www.realtor.com. This is the site promoted by the NAR, and it offers just about every listed home in the country.

TRAP

Most people plan on owning their next home forever. However, statistics suggest that the average time of ownership is only around eight or nine years. If you plan on reselling sooner, you may be willing to accept a less than perfect home choice. You should also look for a home that will more easily resell.

Also check the FSBO (for sale by owner) sites, which may have homes not on www.realtor.com, homes being sold by owners. My favorites include www.owners.com, www.forsalebyowner.com, and www.fsbo.com.

Of course, for most people an agent plays a big role in finding the right home. (Reread Chapter 3 for clues on finding a good agent.) Tell the agent what your priorities are and he or she should begin showing you lots of homes, hopefully most of which will be close to what you really want.

Getting Up to Speed

The important thing here is not to reinvent the wheel. When you begin looking for just the right house, what you're really doing is gathering information. You want to learn which neighborhoods you can afford and in which you feel safe, what those neighborhoods look like, what the traffic and public transportation are like, the quality of schools and shopping, and so forth.

Once you've identified the appropriate neighborhoods, you want to learn about the homes within them. Typically there will be different tracts of homes, each of which may contain half a dozen different models. Hopefully, your agent will know all of them and, after a few days of touring homes, you'll begin to identify them as well.

Soon you'll know which you're interested in and which will most closely fit your needs. As I said, you're gathering information and narrowing the field.

TIP

Always, always carry a map with you. When a broker says that the Maple Heights and Laurel Park areas are affordable, ask for the price range of those areas and then mark it on your map. You'll be surprised how 10 minutes later you can't remember whether it was Maple Park or Laurel Heights or whatever. When you see schools or malls or public transportation on the Internet, mark them on a map. Unless you're very familiar with the area, the information will be gone in moments.

Search on Your Own

Once you've whittled down the general areas that fit your priorities and homes that are close to what you want, whether with an agent or just using the Internet, I suggest you pull back and regroup. Now, take the time to go out on your own and just drive or walk the streets.

This advice comes from a bad mistake a couple made many years ago when buying the first home for their family. They went out with an agent and found an apparently near perfect home. However, they only went there with the agent, never alone. And he always drove there along the same route.

They quickly bought the home. Then, the first week after they moved in, they walked around the neighborhood. It was a dump. There were weed-strewn lawns, garbage on the sidewalk, cars being worked on in driveways, noise, graffiti, and on and on. Of course, they had never seen this before the purchase because the agent carefully drove to the house through the best streets in the area, avoiding the bad ones. Yes, that couple was my wife and I and it was our first home. It was a very long time ago and, fortunately, we've never made that mistake again. (Fortunately, we were able to quickly resell, and for a small profit.)

Become familiar with the neighborhoods where you are considering purchasing. Drive all around them. You should look at how people keep up their properties. Are all the lawns nicely mowed? Or are there broken cars and auto parts strewn across lawns? Watch for broken fences, scattered trash, and graffiti—sure signs the neighborhood is going downhill and may be unsafe. Check the public transportation. Stop at the bus or train station and talk to people. Find out how long it really takes to commute.

Rely on yourself for this. Remember, you're your best advocate.

Choosing a Good Neighborhood

- **Good schools.** Check test scores available at the district office.
- **Low crime rate.** Check with police department's public affairs officer for crime statistics by neighborhood and block.
- **Pride of ownership.** Look to see that all the homes are well kept.
- **Amenities.** Check for parks, wide streets, tall trees, cul-de-sacs, distance to schools and shopping.
- **Balance.** Look for a mix of homes, apartments, condos, townhouses, and so that produces diversity—a good place to live.
- **Anchored.** Look for a neighborhood that has few homes for sale and no detracting new influence (such as a commercial or industrial park coming in nearby).

Once you've winnowed down the areas even more on the basis of items you discovered by driving around, stop, park your car, and start walking. Talk to anyone you meet. Ask about problems in the area, about schools, about good and bad neighbors. When you're doing this, you can also ask if people know of any house not yet listed that might be coming on the market soon. It could be your opportunity to contact the sellers before they list—and potentially get a bargain.

TRAP

Don't be the sort of person who shops only by car. Probably the biggest mistake that buyers make when checking out an area is not walking it. Nothing substitutes for shank's mare when it comes to discovering the kind of neighborhood you're in.

How Do You Find a Specific House?

By now you should have narrowed down the neighborhoods. You can afford and want to live between Ethel Street and Oak Boulevard or in the Pinewood or Horizon Hills or Wildfield tracts. You're ready to find the house. What you need to do is to quickly get a handle on every for-sale house in your price range in those areas.

Isn't that an overwhelming task?

Not really. Be aware that in most areas, 90 percent or more of the homes (including bank-owned foreclosures) are listed with agents. So, go to an agent. If you haven't already done this, have an agent show you the listed houses (including foreclosures) in the area you're considering.

Can You Find Properties before They Are Listed?

There is another category of property that, though rarer, offers potentially greater financial opportunities to you, the buyer. We touched on it earlier; it's a property that has not yet come onto the market.

Sellers have a world of reasons for selling. Sometimes it is a well-thought-out decision determined over a long period of time. In other cases a sudden event such as job change, illness or death, financial reversal, mortgage reset, foreclosure, or something else may cause a quick decision to sell.

Regardless of how it happens, there is always a period of time between when sellers make the decision (or are close to making the decision) and when the property is listed with an agent. I call this the "golden time."

How Do You Find "Golden Time" Homes?

During the golden time, the sellers are willing to sell, but haven't yet fully committed to an agent or anyone else. If you can come in at that point with a reasonable offer, the sellers are more likely to accept. They will be thinking about all the hassles of selling that you will save them. No agents to deal with. No commission to pay. No time spent showing the property and waiting for buyers. You're a life-saver if you come during that golden period.

Unfortunately, the golden time lasts only a few days to a few weeks. Also unfortunately, it's very hard to learn about sellers who are in that golden time. Often it's only through walking the neighborhood or through friends or acquaintances or associates at work that you may learn that Jim is considering selling his home or Mary is planning to list her property.

When you do learn of this, however, act immediately. Contact Mary or Jim that very day or evening at the latest. Tell them you are actively looking to buy a home and would very much like to consider theirs. Will they just let you come over and look?

Then go look.

Chances are the house won't be right. The location may be terrible. Or the home may be too small or too big or too crazy. But every once in a while, it's just right. When it is, strike a deal right there and then.

Presumably by this time you've looked enough to know what houses are going for in the area and you know what a good price is. Come to terms and have your agent or attorney handle the paperwork. (Pay just for the work done, not a full commission.)

By getting to a house before it gets listed or goes up for sale, you can often save a lot of money and get superior terms.

You should also at least consider a fixer-upper, a home that is selling for less because it needs repair work, as well as a FSBO, homes offered directly be sellers. Sometimes you can find a sweet deal here. Check Chapters 12 and 13 for details on how to find these.

Beware of Overbuilt Homes!

You're looking at a house in a neighborhood that typically has three- and four-bedroom, single-story homes. Suddenly you come across a house with two stories and six bedrooms. Chances are that the owner has added on. There's an extra bath, a remodeled kitchen, more bedrooms. In fact, the house looks like a palace. And the price is palatial too!

Nevertheless, it offers so much that you're thinking of some way that you can get into it. Sell the car, the boat, the dog? Work an extra two jobs? Anything to get this wonderful house.

Forget it. The house most likely is a loser, a white elephant. The only reason it looks so terrific is that it's a BMW surrounded by Fords. Put it with other BMWs and Mercedes and Rolls-Royces and it'll look common.

There are relatively few things that an owner can do to add on to a house and still recoup the money invested. Remodeling a kitchen is one. But start adding floors and rooms and very quickly the house becomes overbuilt—the neighborhood doesn't justify the work that's done . . . or the price required.

Typically in such a situation, the owners are asking far less than the actual costs of the remodeling that they spent, but far more than surrounding houses cost. It's going to take them a very long time to find a buyer. And if you're that buyer, it's going to take you a very long time when you want to resell.

Buyers (like you) look for location first, the building second. If a house is too big or overbuilt for a location, it becomes a problem. You don't want to purchase someone else's problem.

TIP

Buy the least expensive house in the most expensive neighborhood you can afford. If you do, you multiply your chances for making money later on when you resell.

How to Avoid Buyer's Burnout

As you go from house to house looking to find just the right one, remember that a big factor is exhaustion. It's not just being physically tired. It's the fact that after a while, all the houses start to look the same. Therefore it's a good idea to keep in mind the following:

- Always take a notepad and map with you when you tour houses with an agent. Mark the location of the house on the map and write down special features on the pad. If the owner offers you a fact sheet, save it even if you don't seem interested in the house at the time. Later on, you may think about it and realize the home had more appeal than you at first realized.

- Never look at more than five or six houses in any one session. After that, you're no longer being careful. You're just running through not paying attention to the details that could make you fall in love with a place. If you need to see a lot of houses, take big breaks. See three in the morning, then stop and have lunch. See three more, then stop and do something else. See three more in the early evening. Nine houses in one day is the absolute capacity of almost any prospective buyer. Even with nine, the features of one will begin to blend in with the features of another.

- Use a digital camera to snap a picture of each house that appeals to you. A picture *is* worth a thousand words. You'll instantly remember the features of a house once you see a picture of the outside or some room inside. Frequently, agents or owners will provide you with photocopied pictures as well.

- Sketch floor plans that you like on your notepad. It helps to remember and is also a good means of comparing one house with another.

- Don't be afraid to ask questions. Many buyers worry that they'll be thought foolish if they ask about drain pipes or washrooms or taxes or something they think everyone else knows about. There are no foolish questions, only foolish buyers who don't ask questions. A seemingly simple question may open up a whole line of concern that you weren't aware of.

TIP

It's far better to ask and learn about the problems of a house *before* you buy than to be stuck with them *after* you own it.

How Do You Know What the House Is Worth?

Market value in residential real estate is determined by comparing what's for sale with what's sold—looking at the market. If a house in a tract sold for $250,000 a month ago and the nearly identical house next door is now for sale, it's a pretty good guess that it, too, is worth around $250,000. (Of course, if the market's falling you'll want to discount the price—if it's rising, you'll want to add to it.)

Once you find a house you are interested in, ask to see a CMA or Comparable Market Analysis. Any good real estate agent can very quickly prepare a list of all the similar homes that have sold over the past six months to a year.

Or you can compose such a list yourself. Check out www.zillow.com for prices of comparable homes. To get an online CMA for a fee (or sometimes to have a real estate agent call), check out www.reiclub.com, www.homevalue.com, and www.home again.com.

Check out the comps. Subtract for features your subject house lacks. Add for extras your subject house has. For example, if the house that sold for $250,000 didn't have a pool and the house you are interested in does, add value for the pool. (Pools add to the price, but not much—it may cost $50,000 to put a pool in, but it may only add $10,000 to the home's price at sale time.) To learn how much the pool adds to your subject home, try to find other sales of similar homes with pools.

TRAP

When looking at a CMA keep in mind that no two homes are ever exactly the same, no two lots (sites) ever have exactly the same view, size, or quiet location, and the condition of every house varies at least a little.

What About Foreclosures?

With so many foreclosures on the market in recent years, it's only natural that home buyers would wonder if they presented an opportunity. After all, if you can buy a good foreclosure that meets your housing needs and get it at a fraction of the price of a standard resale or new home, why not go for it? I've never known anyone who was pleased to pay more than they could for anything by buying at retail—why not buy at wholesale, even a house?

The most important tip about foreclosures that I can convey, however, is that there's nothing magic about the word. Yes, foreclosure means that some borrower is losing his or her property to a lender. But, given the down market in which most foreclosures occur, it may very well be that the big reason the property is being lost is that the mortgage is higher than the home's market value. In other words, the foreclosure could be no bargain at all. Instead it might even be a more expensive property than comparable listings nearby.

TRAP

Don't equate all foreclosures with bargains. Some are. Some definitely are not.

That doesn't mean that there aren't foreclosure bargains out there—there definitely are. However, you have to know what to look for and be very careful when you purchase. In this chapter we'll look at three areas where you as a home buyer can find foreclosure bargains:

- Preforeclosures
- Auctions
- REOs (Real Estate Owned—held for sale by a lender)

Preforeclosures

There are three steps to the foreclosure process. (Actually four. The real first step begins when the borrower stops making the mortgage payments.) Foreclosure officially starts when the lender records a Notice of Default. Typically this is done after the borrower has not made full mortgage payments for a number of months. (How long before the lender files is at its discretion.)

Once the lender files the Notice, the borrower is said to be in "preforeclosure." The process has started. However, now the borrower has some time before it concludes. The actual time varies by state. In California, which uses a deed-of-trust, this period lasts about $3\frac{1}{2}$ months. In othyer states, such as Florida, which uses a mortgage instrument that must be foreclosed through court action, it can take longer.

During this time, the borrower can make good the mortgage by paying all back interest, penalties, and fees.

Alternatively, the borrower can refinance to a new loan to get out of foreclosure (something most borrowers try to do, but are not successful at). Or the borrower can sell the property. That's where you come in.

When you find a borrower in preforeclosure, you can buy the property, but typically you must get your own financing to replace the mortgage that's in foreclosure. (The lender will most likely *not* allow you to assume the existing mortgage and will not want to refinance it, preferring instead to be fully rid of the property.)

When the Borrower Is Upside Down

During the foreclosure panic of 2007 and 2008, the problem was that most borrowers couldn't refinance or resell because they were "upside down." That means they owed more than the property was worth.

If you wanted to buy their property, you would have to negotiate not only with the borrower (seller), but also with the lender for a "short sale." Here, the lender accepts less than is owed in order to be rid of the house. It usually takes some sharp negotiating to get a lender to go for this.

The Role of Home Buyer versus Investor

From our very brief discussion, what should be apparent is that in order to buy a preforeclosure you're going to need to:

1. Find the property
2. Negotiate to purchase it directly with the borrower/seller
3. Probably negotiate a short sale face-to-face with the lender

Sometimes (not always, but occasionally) a buyer can get a good deal here by cutting the price way down with the lender. However, it takes a lot of negotiating skill. Thus, most preforeclosures are bought by investors. Most home buyers simply don't want the bother and aren't prepared for the work or to spend the time involved.

TRAP

To prevent unscrupulous speculators from taking advantage of borrowers in pre-foreclosure, some states have enacted redemption laws. These allow the borrower to redeem the property for a period of time (sometimes as long as a year or more) after it is purchased. During that redemption period the buyer may not be able to fix up or resell the property.

If you would like to investigate buying preforeclosures in more detail, I suggest you look into my White Paper that explains it. This can be found on my Web site, www.robertirwin.com.

Buying a Home at Auction

There are two kinds of auctions commonly conducted in real estate these days, although most home buyers don't really understand the distinction.

Foreclosure Auction

The first is the foreclosure auction. After statutory time has run out for the borrower in preforeclosure, the lender auctions off the house "on the courthouse steps" to the highest bidder. (In trust deed states, the trustee does the auctioning; in judicial foreclosure states, it's typically the sheriff.)

Anyone can bid. However, the lender normally bids the full amount of the mortgage plus accrued interest, penalties, and fees. Thus, you usually have to bid higher than the lender to buy the home.

These foreclosure auctions are fraught with peril for the inexperienced or unwary bidder. A few problems are:

- Usually there is no title insurance (as there normally is with a conventional purchase). Thus the bidder may not be aware of whether the mortgage is a first, a second, or a fifth. (The order is critical to determining payoffs.) You could buy the home, paying off the foreclosing mortgage, only to discover that a higher mortgage(s) was still on the property. You could end up throwing your money away.
- There's typically little to no opportunity to inspect the property, thus it could be severely damaged and require extensive and costly renovation; you wouldn't know.
- These sales are for cash, so you must line up your new financing well in advance, something that can be difficult to do.

For these, as well as other reasons, I do *not* suggest that the average home buyer consider purchasing a property at a foreclosure auction. If you're an experienced investor who has agents and attorneys advising you, it's a different story. If you just want a home to live in, my suggestion is that you stay away. Yes, you could pick up a terrific bargain. But just as likely (probably more likely!), you'd lose your money.

Seller's Auctions

The second type is the seller's auction. This is a different kind of auction and it comes in a variety of forms. The most common is where a group of sellers (sometimes including lenders) will pool their homes with an auction company which will then conduct a public auction. You've probably seen these advertised in your local newspaper. (Other forms involve an individual owner auctioning off his or her one house, conducting a contest to find buyers, and so on.)

The auction is typically held in a big tent. There may be snacks and even champagne. Usually there is a lot of hoopla associated with the auction.

The auction company handling the sale is usually very careful to point out that everything is on the "up and up." They typically offer title insurance and an escrow, and may even have their own lender(s) for financing. You register by coming up with a cashier's check for a set amount (perhaps $1,000), signing a few documents, and then the bidding begins.

Can you get a bargain at these seller's auctions?

It all depends on what you consider a bargain. Yes, in a falling market you probably can buy a house at far less than the old market price (before the downturn). On the other hand, your purchase price might not be much lower, if at all, than the current market price.

It's important to understand that the true function of such auctions is *not* to provide you with bargains. It's to get the homes sold at the highest possible price for the sellers.

TIP

Find out if the auction is "absolute" or "reserve."

The key to these seller's auctions is to find out if they are "absolute" or "reserve." An absolute auction means that the houses will be sold to the highest bidder, no matter how low the price. If someone only bids $1,000, then that's what the house will sell for.

In a reserve auction, the seller reserves the right to refuse to sell below a certain price (which may or may not be made public). Thus, if the highest bid is $1,000, the seller can say that he, she, or it (if a lender) refuses to sell because the bid didn't come up to the minimum, which might be $100,000.

What should be obvious is that you can really catch a bargain at an absolute auction. You are far less likely to do so at a reserve auction.

Nearly all seller's auctions that I've observed have been reserve. Usually the reserve of each house is kept high enough to make sure the seller doesn't lose money. (Occasionally one house, typically a real dog, will be sold at a very low reserve as a "loss leader.")

It would be incorrect to say that seller's auctions are manipulated. Everything is out in the open, if you know what questions to ask and what to look for. The auctioneers are usually willing to tell you if the auction is reserve or absolute and whether or not they will let you know the reserve price(s). (Some states require auctioneers to make public the amount of the reserve, others don't.)

From the above discussion, you can probably guess that my own personal opinion is that most seller's auctions are a waste of my time. I would definitely go to an absolute auction. I wouldn't bother with one that was reserve.

Lender Owned Property

The final step in the foreclosure process is when the lender buys the property at a foreclosure auction (noted above—not a lender's auction) and now owns it. (These are called REOs or Real Estate Owned.)

Of course the lender doesn't really want to own property. Its business is lending money. When it owns property it's considered a liability and frequently ties up the lender's precious capital reserves. Thus, the lender's goal is to dump the REOs.

Unfortunately, most property in foreclosure is neglected and in dire straits. It typically needs heavy repairs.

So the first thing the lender does is to get a team out there to fix up the property. Then, it usually lists it with an agent (to whom it pays a commission) and tries to sell it at market price.

How Do You Buy REOs?

There are undoubtedly brokers in your area who handle REOs for lenders. You can find them by using the Web sites noted at the end of this chapter. Or you can check your local newspaper. The agents often advertise that they have foreclosed properties for sale.

The purchase of a REO is handled in the same way as buying a conventional home from a seller. You make an offer. There may be counteroffers. If there's a sale, escrow is opened, you get title insurance, a new mortgage, a home inspection, disclosures, and so on. (The disclosures are typically worthless since the owner is a lender who probably knows nothing about the physical attributes of the property and, hence, has nothing to disclose.)

Can you get a bargain by buying a REO?

Again, yes and no. The lender is trying to sell the property for maximum dollars, at or as close to market value as possible. Hence, the asking price for REOs is rarely a bargain price.

On the other hand, you can lowball the seller/lender. And, in a down market where the seller/lender may have 1,500 similar REOs for sale dragging down its stock value, tying up capital reserves, and catching the eye of federal regulators, it may be keen to sell quickly. Thus, you may have a better chance of getting a quick, low, bargain price than you have with an individual seller trying to dispose of one home.

TRAP

In a market full of REOs, it's often hard to get a lender to consider a lowball offer because it has so many REOs on its plate that it simply doesn't have the time or human resources to respond.

On the other hand, to find out, you may need to make lots of lowball offers on many different houses, before you find a lender hungry enough to take one.

The Clean Sale

To my way of thinking, the typical REO purchase is the cleanest foreclosure deal the average home buyer is likely to get. Usually the homes are fixed up. (You may be able to swing a real steal by buying a REO from a lender before it's fixed up.)

You may get the benefit of working with an agent. There's normally escrow, title insurance, professional inspection, and so on. In other words, it's very much like a conventional deal, with all the usual protections that offers.

If you're looking to buy a foreclosure and don't want the hassles of dealing with a preforeclosure, or the risks of buying at auction, I suggest you consider the REO. It's the cleanest deal of its kind you're likely to get.

Find out more about foreclosures at online sites such as www. foreclosure.com or www.realtytrac.com.

Negotiating to Win

N egotiating is like wooing a lover—almost anything goes.

When you buy a home, everything, with only rare exceptions, is up for grabs. How much you grab for yourself and how much the seller grabs depends on how well you negotiate.

TIP

There's just one thing to remember when it comes to negotiating real estate—*everything is negotiable!*

Here's a *partial* list of what's negotiable when you buy a house:

What's Negotiable When You Buy a Home

- Price
- Financing
- Closing costs (except where specified by law)

- Occupancy (when you'll get the key and can move in)
- Painting (will the seller repaint a portion of or the entire house?)
- Repairs (will the seller repair the roof, plumbing, windows, and so on, and what kind and quality of repairs will be made?)
- Yard (will the seller remove unwanted trees or bushes, or put in desired landscaping?)
- Fixtures (which lights, fans, and appliances stay and which go?)
- Wall coverings (do the drapes stay or go?)
- Doghouse (does it go or stay?)
- Dog or cat (does it stay?)
- Furniture (will the seller throw in certain pieces?)
- Closing costs (will the seller pay yours?)
- And everything else!

The great problem, however, is that most buyers feel at a loss as negotiators. Many people, in the back of their minds, know they're going to come out second best. So they give up before even beginning. That's the trap.

That's also a shame because negotiation gives the buyer incredible power in making a favorable transaction. Of course, it can also place him or her in a position of immense weakness. The fact is that how you negotiate determines whether you get the home of your dreams at a great price—or whether those dreams end up being an overpriced nightmare.

Do You Negotiate from Weakness?

I once had a friend who had a strong dislike for traveling in Mexico, even though her business obligations required that she routinely go to such places. "Why?" I asked her on one occasion. "The people are very friendly. The scenery in many areas is spectacular. And the currency exchange rate for Americans is often favorable. So what don't you like about it?" She glowered at me for a moment, then replied, "You seldom know what the price of anything is." She waited for that to sink in, then continued, "You want to buy a pair of shoes. The price written on them is one thing. But you just know you should be able to get them for less, maybe half of that price if you haggle.

"But the moment you try to bargain, the seller gets upset and starts protesting, sometimes even accusing you of trying to steal food from the mouths of his children.

"He says you're trying to cheat him and demands the full price. I get embarrassed. I end up paying full price, sometimes even more just to get away! Why don't they just put the real price out there to begin with?"

I nodded understandingly and said, "But don't you see? The negotiation for the price is a kind of ritual. It's anticipated that you'll offer less and pay less than the asking price. The seller's insults and threats are just a way of doing business, trying to get you to pay more. *There's nothing personal in it.* Most people enjoy the negotiation."

She shook her head, then said, "I guess I'm just no good at negotiating."

I indicated that when I'd once visited Mexico, I'd seen a buyer and seller haggle for nearly half an hour over the price of some small trinket, hurling accusations of thievery and insults relating to family origin. All the hostility was immediately forgotten the moment the sale was concluded, at which time both buyer and seller embraced each other as though they were bosom buddies. "Negotiation for price and even terms of sale is the accepted practice throughout most of the world. It is an ancient and honored tradition."

My friend scowled at me. "It's not a tradition in the United States. When I go into a department store, I know what the price is. There are no shenanigans, no arguing, no negotiations. If a pair of shoes in Macy's is listed at $85, that's the price—no ifs, ands, or buts!"

I nodded and thought about the last time I was in Macy's and bought a sweater. The full market price was $60. But it was half off because of a sale. And because I was there early on a Saturday I could take another 25 percent off. And if I opened a credit card, it was another 10 percent off . . . And on and on.

It was the end of our conversation. My friend was absolutely convinced that negotiating was the bane of doing business.

How wrong she was.

Negotiation is alive and well everywhere including in the United States. No, you probably won't recognize it openly when you go to most stores, although it is reflected in sales and cut-rate prices. On the other hand, it is most clearly seen when you buy high ticket items, like a car, or rare coins, or paintings, or . . . real estate. Negotiation for price or terms of sale always has been and probably always will be the *rule* in any capitalist society. It's how true market price is discovered.

How Do You Successfully Negotiate in Real Estate?

Which brings us back to buying a home. Here, everything is negotiable—the most important items usually being the price and the terms. If you're a good negotiator, you may end up paying 5 to 30 percent or more below what the seller is asking. Negotiation is an inherent part of buying real estate and if you're going to participate, you should plan on learning the basic skills.

Should You Rely on the Agent?

At this point, I'm sure some readers are saying, "Hold on. I worked with an agent when I bought my last home. The agent did my negotiating. The agent saw that I got a good price."

Maybe. You may have gotten a good price, but if you did, my guess is that it probably was because of your own efforts. The agent in many cases, even if it's a buyer's agent and not a seller's, will only negotiate hard enough to make the minimum deal that you'll accept. Do you remember telling your agent you wanted a low price? And did the agent suggest you were unlikely to get that low price, but if you offered just a bit more, that higher price would more likely be accepted?

After all, the higher your agent can get you to offer, the easier it is for him or her to get the seller to accept. Ask a really low price and many agents simply won't even take in the offer! They'll tell you it's ridiculous. They won't fight for you.

Also, the lower your offer, the less chance there is of getting a commission. Remember, the agent normally gets a commission only when there's a sale. The higher your offer, the more chance the seller might be willing to accept it. A sale quickly made is a commission earned.

So instead of offering $25,000 less than the asking price, perhaps you offer $5,000 less—and get it. The seller is happy. The agent's happy.

And you, you big dummy, are happy because you think you got yourself a "good price."

Who Can You Rely On?

This doesn't mean that all agents don't fight for you. In my experience many agents do.

However, the point is that you shouldn't rely on anyone but yourself when it comes to negotiation. A good agent can handle the actual mechanics of speaking for you to the seller, and that's certainly a big plus. But the agent can't or at least shouldn't tell you what to offer.

It's ultimately up to you to determine what the parameters of the negotiation are going to be. You set the price, the terms, and all the other conditions of sale that you will accept. (Also see Chapter 4 for picking a good *buyer's* agent.)

Are You Your Own Worst Enemy?

Which brings us back to you. Most house hunters, particularly house hunters who don't regularly invest in real estate, are worried about hurting the seller's feelings, about insulting the agent by offering a price far lower than the asking price, and most important, about doing anything that would appear foolish.

If that's the way you feel when you open negotiations for the purchase of your next home, you are a gone goose.

Remember the example of buying shoes in Mexico? The seller and buyer in Mexico often argue back and forth for a long time, haggling over the price. But then, when it's all said and done, they shake hands and become bosom buddies.

Well, you may not end up bosom buddies with the seller, but remember that when negotiating for real estate you are participating in that same age-old ritual of bargaining. You are relying on your own cleverness and personal willpower.

If you are weak and susceptible to the influence of the seller (or the seller's agent), you could be talked into paying a higher price, getting less favorable terms, or (worst of all) accepting a house that you really don't want. On the other hand, if you are a good "horse trader" you are going to get a good deal all around.

Can You Learn to Negotiate Successfully?

In the old days in real estate (by old days I mean as late as the 1950s) the Latin expression "caveat emptor" was often quoted: "Let the buyer beware." Since that time, consumer protection laws have swelled to the point where today the buyer who knows how to take advantage of these laws is protected and even has advantages as never before.

However, when it comes to the actual negotiations, there are no protections for the buyer. You are at your own peril. You can make a good deal. Or you can get yourself into terrible trouble.

The question naturally arises, therefore, of how a person who is not a real estate professional can negotiate successfully in what may be a den of wolves. How do you avoid cheating yourself by your negotiation inexperience?

The answer is by acquiring knowledge. Having read this chapter thus far, you've already acquired a great deal that you may not have known before. You now know that everything is negotiable. When the agent says, "There's no way you can ask for the refrigerator. It's personal property and goes with the sellers automatically." You can stand back, catch your breath, and say with confidence, "Either I get that damn refrigerator or there's no deal!" Grumbling, the agent will write into the contract that the refrigerator goes with the house, knowing full well that he or she is going to have to fight the sellers for hours to get them to agree.

You should now know that there's nothing embarrassing about submitting low offers and making your agent struggle to get the seller to sign. There's nothing wrong with insisting on terms which are totally favorable to you. You should also now know that it's a mistake to let a seller's agent "assist" you in determining the price to offer. If you're going to get assistance, be sure it's from a buyer's agent.

Finally, you should now know that there's nothing foolish about getting down on the ground and scrambling for price and terms.

It's an ancient tradition that, regardless of your particular background, is your human heritage. You were born to do it!

Knowledge Is Power

Ultimately, how you fare when buying a home is going to be a direct result of the knowledge you have. The more you know about the condition of the house, the motivation of the seller, the state of the market, and the art of negotiation, the better a position you'll be in to negotiate from strength.

TIP

The best way to negotiate is to negotiate from strength. There is only one way to get strength: through knowledge.

Here are some quick tips for negotiating from strength that you may find particularly helpful:

Tips for Negotiating

- **Never be insulting.** Remember, it's only business. If you insult an agent or seller, you can turn it into a personal fight, which you'll probably lose.
- **Get time on your side.** Give the sellers very little time to make a decision, perhaps 12 to 24 hours or less. It forces them to choose and helps prevent a better offer from slipping in.
- *Appear* **"hard nosed."** If you convince your agent you won't pay any more (even if you will), he or she will more likely be able to convince the seller.
- **Find out the seller's motivation.** If the house is in foreclosure, the seller is out of work, has been transferred, there's a divorce, or the seller otherwise must move quickly, consider a lowball offer. A desperate seller should be willing to give you a better deal.
- **Be willing to compromise (counteroffer).** But only when you're absolutely sure you can't get your original offer.

- **If you can't get your price, try to get your terms.** Sellers are often hung up on price. If you give them their price, they may be willing to carry back a low-interest-rate mortgage, include lots of personal property, let you have early possession, or almost anything else that you might need, which may be worth more than price to you.

Can You Negotiate on a New House?

Of course. Sometimes you're buying a brand new home instead of a resale. The builder/developer has a set price written in ink on the brochure. Either you pay that price, you are told, or you don't get the home. Right?

Not in a cold market. When the market is hot people will sometimes camp out in front of builder/developers' offices for days just for the privilege of paying full price for a new home. On the other hand, when there's a real estate recession, builders can't get rid of their new homes. They'll consider any offer, no matter how ridiculous is seems to you.

Just keep in mind that builder/developers often have a relatively small profit margin and they may not be able to accept a severely reduced price. (See Chapter 14 on buying a brand new home from a builder/developer.)

Should You Negotiate Directly with the Seller?

Sometimes sellers will bypass the use of an agent and attempt to sell their homes themselves. (In the trade these are called FSBOs— for sale by owners.) The temptation is to think that because no agent is involved, the seller doesn't have to pay a commission and, hence, can offer a lower price. (In truth, many FSBOs actually want *more* for their home than market price.)

Maybe you'll be able to get a FSBO for less. On the other hand, you now not only have to set the parameters of your negotiations (price and terms) but also have to carry those negotiations out face-to-face.

If you're a good horse trader and if the seller is too, things should go fine and no agent may be needed. But, unfortunately, in our country most people have been inured into thinking in terms of fixed prices and not negotiation. Hence, when you offer the FSBO seller far less than he or she is asking, even though a reasonable price from your perspective, you could be asked to leave in not so pleasant terms and further negotiations may be impossible.

Or, if the seller is a good negotiator and you aren't, when your low offer is rejected along with suggestions that you've insulted the seller's integrity, you may be put off and leave without realizing that it was all part of the game.

As a result, for the majority of people, buying face-to-face from sellers can be more difficult. (I'll have a lot more to say about buying directly from a seller in Chapter 13.)

How Do You Get Started with the Negotiations?

Find a house and make an offer. Or, as those in the business know, a counteroffer. We'll go into this in detail in the next chapter.

For more information on negotiating, check out my book *Tips and Traps When Negotiating Real Estate*, Second Edition (McGraw-Hill, 2006).

What Should You Offer?

Unlike buying an item in a grocery store, in real estate the price is only the "asking price." You can pay it. Or you can offer any other price you'd like to pay.

I've never heard of a buyer who boasted about paying *more* than a seller was asking. Many buyers, however, love to boast about paying far *less*. We all want to get the lowest price we can, a price that we feel makes the property a good value at the least, a bargain at best.

But how do we achieve that?

If you ask your agent, as noted in the last chapter, you may meet resistance. Most agents would prefer an easy negotiation, which means that you come in at close to full asking price. (Remember, an agent doesn't normally get paid unless there's a sale.) In addition, the agent may be working for the seller (unless you're using a dual or buyer's agent) and may not owe you allegiance.

Consequently, in many ways when you ask your real estate agent how much to offer, you may be in a position similar to asking an automobile salesperson how much to offer. You're asking the wrong person. You're, in effect, asking the seller, or at the least someone who's more interested in getting *any* deal than a really good deal for you.

Whom should you ask?

Rely on Yourself

If you've been looking at homes for a while, by now you should have a pretty good idea what similar houses are listed for. This should give you a good idea of the price range you should be considering in an offer.

TRAP

Selling prices and listing prices are usually different. In most markets, homes sell for less, sometimes much less, than listed.

Be sure you check the comps (the prices comparable homes have recently sold for). Use the Internet or ask your agent to let you see the selling prices of similar homes going back at least six months. Any agent worth her salt has these figures readily available from the MLS (Multiple Listing Service).

Pick out all sales for similar houses, then try to get as close a match as possible (same number of bedrooms, bathrooms, pool, amenities, and so on). In an active market you should find half a dozen sales or more.

Extra features such as a new kitchen or bathroom or other remodeling add to the value of a house. However, they don't normally make the house significantly more valuable than its neighbors.

Any house that's priced more than 10 percent above its neighbors because of improvements may be a "white elephant." It may be overimproved.

Don't feel sorry for sellers who have sunk a ton of money into remodeling and are now trying to get every penny back from you. That's their problem. Don't make it yours.

How Much Should You Offer?

Sellers in most markets ask more than they are willing to take for their homes. They are expecting to come down some, hence the above-market asking price. If you pay what the seller is asking, you could be wasting money. The real trick is knowing how much less than asking price a seller will take.

Sometimes a seller will only come down a few thousand dollars. Other times they may drop 10 percent or more. And, of course, there's that occasional seller who refuses to come down a dime.

Unless you've got supernatural powers (or the seller's agent spills the beans), you won't know. That means you have to learn through the negotiating process. Your offer and each counteroffer the seller makes tell you more. Eventually, if you're a good negotiator, you will have gotten the lowest possible price.

Should You "Lowball" the Seller?

In a cold market like we've recently had, it often starts out with a low bid. Remember, you can't very well go lower after you've previously made a high bid; you would lose credibility and the seller's interest.

However, if you bid too low initially, the seller may not believe that you're in earnest in buying the property and may simply turn your offer down without even a counter. Which brings up the biggest risk when lowballing: you may lose the property entirely.

Now it's a matter of understanding yourself. If you're looking at this property more as a home than as an investment, you may not want to risk losing it. You may feel that you'll simply die if you don't get it. You just *can't* lose it!

TIP

From an investment perspective, it's better to lowball 10 houses and not get any of them, than to pay too much for one house.

But if you feel this house is the home you can't live without, then don't bother with lowball offers. They're simply too risky for you. Come in close to full price, so that this one won't get away.

TRAP

Are you more investor or more habitat buyer? Are you in love with the property? Or can you just walk away? Are you willing to make offers on a dozen properties before getting one? Or is the whole process so overwhelming that you simply want to get it over with? How you answer these questions should guide how low—or high—an offer you make.

How Much Should You Lowball?

You may want to offer as much as 25 percent or more less than the asking price, especially in a down market. However, usually that's just a test offer, trying to see what the water is like. In all but a very cold market, a seller's likely to simply reject it out of hand. Indeed, the seller may simply ignore the offer and not counter it and that could mean the end of the deal for you. Often the goal of the initial lowball is to get a counteroffer from the seller. Try to offer enough to entice the seller to at least respond, to at least make a counteroffer.

What If the Seller Counteroffers?

Counteroffers occur when the seller turns down your original offer, but then sends you back a sales agreement that offers different price, terms, or virtually anything else that departs from your original offer. It is at this point that negotiations begin in earnest. How well you respond to the seller's counteroffer with your own counter (or acceptance) determines the quality of the deal you'll get.

> **TIP**
> Experienced real estate investors often say that in reality, buying real estate isn't the art of making an offer. It's the art of counteroffering.

Some very savvy buyers will purposely make lowball offers in the hope that the sellers will counter, perhaps at a price lower than the buyer is willing to pay! If not, these savvy buyers hope to engage the sellers in sometimes protracted negotiations in the hope of eventually wearing them down and getting a much better price or much better terms.

How Do You Read the Counteroffer?

A counteroffer is usually a good sign. (Of course, it's a better sign if the seller accepts your original offer!) A counter means the seller is willing to dicker with you. After a seller counters at a significantly lower price (but not as low as you've originally offered), you've really got only three alternatives (besides simply walking away):

1. Accept the seller's counter, if you think it's low enough.
2. Compromise and counter somewhere between your original offer and the seller's first counteroffer.
3. Repeat your original offer, if you think it's a good price.

Compromising at between the seller's last offer and your original offer (#2 above), may land the deal. Or the seller may cut the remaining distance in half again with yet another counter. Or again the seller may simply pick up his or her marbles and leave the game. If the seller does counter, however, you're probably well along toward getting the home at a reasonable price.

Sticking to your original offer (reoffering it as your first counter), has some negotiating drawbacks. It tells the seller to take it or leave it. It says you're not willing to compromise. A certain percentage of the time (no one knows how much, but it's not high), you'll win by holding pat. The seller will indeed capitulate and accept your original offer. This usually only happens, however, in a cold market and with a desperate seller.

More often the seller will simply throw up his or her hands and say there's no dealing with you. The seller will then simply walk away. After all, if you don't raise your offer, what choice have you left the seller but to take your offer, or quit?

My suggestion is that unless you think your original lowball offer is actually realistic, always counter the seller's counter, even if you only come up a thousand dollars or so. It keeps the negotiations open. And gives the seller another chance to come down even more!

Eventually, you'll get the house you want at the price you want to pay. Or you'll move on.

How Do You Make an Offer and a Counteroffer?

Have your agent and/or attorney write it up. Most agents have their own office forms.

TRAP

Unless you're very experienced in real estate, don't attempt to write up your own offers or counters. The language must be precise. If you make a mistake, it could cost you your deal . . . or worse.

Here's the basic procedure, once the offer is written up:

- Have your agent present the offer as soon as possible to the sellers.
- The sellers will either accept the offer exactly as presented or turn it down.
- If the sellers turn down the offer, they can make a counteroffer to you.
- You may now accept their counteroffer exactly as written, or turn it down. If you turn it down, you may counter back.
- This countering can go on almost indefinitely. Sometimes it gets down to arguing over a washing machine or repainting one wall of a living room.
- The deal is made only when both you and the sellers accept exactly the same offer or counter.

TRAP

You can't both accept and counter. Whenever you or the seller counters with any kind of change at all, it is a new offer. Either party now has the option of walking away from the deal, you with your deposit and no strings attached.

The Terrible (Lowball) Offer

As noted, some buyers will purposely make very unfavorable offers to sellers in the hopes they will counter with a compromise offer that is still far below what they were asking. This is a strategy that sometimes works. However, it is also fraught with peril. Remember, the sellers may be insulted by the low offer and simply turn it down out of hand and not counter at all, which could end negotiations. If you accept this risk, however, and the sellers do counter, you could be on the way to a great deal.

The Compromise Offer

If you don't want to risk alienating the sellers right off the bat, then there's the compromise offer. It's higher than the lowball, but still far lower than what the sellers are asking. This is an offer that you're pretty sure will drive the sellers to the negotiating table. It sets the stage for a bargaining process that will get you the property at a price and terms you can afford and are willing to pay.

How do you know what to put into the "compromise offer"? What price, terms, and so forth should it be? Every situation is different. However, the general guidelines are that you try to make the lowest offer to which the sellers will make a *serious* counter. You'll have to judge the sellers' motivation and the market conditions.

The Wonderful Offer

You would only make this offer if you were desperately in love with the home and/or the market was strong. You would offer very close to or right at full price.

You want the sellers to know that you're intent on buying their home, so you make an offer close to asking price. But you're hoping that they will cut you a little slack by either accepting your offer as you've had it written, or countering by taking a little off their original price.

In a normal market, the sellers might indeed accept. Or they might counter, splitting the difference. In a hot market, they might simply counter by reoffering their original price. Or even offering a higher price than they were asking and than you offered! In a cold market if you offer full price, the sellers will likely think they've died and gone to heaven!

Tips for Making Offers and Counteroffers

1. Don't Paint Yourself into a Corner. If you only make terrible offers that favor you, you'll often lose. If you're determined to have the house, you're better off making a counter that contains enough bones for the sellers so that if they don't accept, at least they'll counter back.

2. Keep the Ball in Play. The goal in bargaining is to keep the ball in play. You always want there to be a counteroffer somewhere en route. The moment either you or the sellers stop countering without a full acceptance, the deal is dead.

3. Pay Attention to Timing. When you make an offer to a seller, it is open ended. That means that you've written down the price, the terms, and any other conditions that you want, and that you agree to be bound by them. If the seller accepts and communicates that acceptance to you, you're on the hook.

However, things change. The house you're in love with today may not be so appealing tomorrow. Yet another home may come along that really turns you on next week. Your financial condition could change. Therefore, you don't want to make this open-ended offer last forever.

Further, if you give the seller lots of time to consider your offer, someone else may slip in a better offer. You want to set a time limit on your offer and your counters.

Make your offer for as short a time as practical. Twenty-four hours is not unreasonable. Midnight of the day the offer is presented may not be unreasonable, if the seller can easily be reached. (Be sure to take into consideration how long it will take to contact the seller. But remember, today, almost everyone is reachable by phone, fax, or e-mail.)

4. Don't Let Agents Bully You into Giving Them More Time.
Sometimes agents will encourage you to put in a long period of time—four to five days or even a week—for acceptance to take place. They may say that it will take that long to convince the sellers to sign.

This approach makes sense only if the sellers are out of the country, maybe off the planet! (Remember there are cell phones, fax, Internet, and other forms of instant communication.) Even then it may only be marginally good advice. Remember, the more time the sellers have to think about it, the more time for them to talk themselves out of accepting it. And the more time there is for someone to come in with a better offer. Giving the sellers a lot of time to accept is simply cutting your own throat.

5. Be Prepared to Withdraw Your Offer. It's important to understand that although your offer is open ended (you're committed; the sellers aren't—until they sign), and although it has a defined time limit for acceptance, you do not have to keep it open. Any time before the sellers sign *and that acceptance is conveyed to you,* you can withdraw the offer. You make an offer at 5:00 that the agent will present to the sellers at 8:00. At 8:30, you call the sellers' house and ask the agent if they've accepted. He says he's just presented it and they're thinking about it. They'll probably sign in a few minutes. You instruct him to withdraw the offer immediately. The offer is no longer good.

Why would you want to withdraw an offer? There are lots of reasons. Soon after submitting an offer, you find a better house at a better price. You want out of the offer immediately. Or, perish the thought, you or a family member has a car accident or you discover that you have a debilitating disease and you don't want to go through with the deal. Or you're simply being fickle.

It doesn't matter. You don't have to have a reason. You can withdraw the offer any time before acceptance is communicated to you.

6. Don't Be Confused by Talk from an Agent That the Sellers Have Accepted Your Offer with a Few Minor Changes. Many first-time buyers are unaware of the important subtleties of unaccepted offers. I have seen agents get sellers to make a counteroffer, then call the buyer and say, "Congratulations—your offer was accepted! Only the seller made a few changes that I'll need to drop by and have you initial. I'll explain it to you when I get there."

That's wrong. If the seller changes anything, it's a new offer—totally and completely. A counteroffer is just that. It's a new offer that the seller is making. *You are under no obligation to accept a counteroffer, no matter how close to your original offer it may be.*

7. Sellers Are at Risk Too. Be aware that sellers are at great risk when they make counteroffers. This is so because they are, in effect, rejecting your offer and substituting another for it. When this happens, the tables are turned. The sellers may give you a time limit to accept their counteroffer and you can do with it what you will. (Just remember, if you counter the counter, once again the ball's in the other court.)

8. Keep to the Same Document When Possible. It is good strategy to make the counteroffer (either your own or the sellers') on the same document as the original offer. The reason is psychological. When the sellers counter on the same document, even though you may know that their counter rejects your original offer, using the same document makes it somehow seem like you're closer than before. When you counter the sellers' counteroffer, putting it on the same document does the same thing for the sellers.

Some agents use sales agreements that have a separate section on the last page which reads, "Seller's Counteroffer." The idea here is that this is the designated place for the sellers to write in their counter.

I think this is a bad idea. It encourages sellers to think that a counteroffer is warranted. A sales agreement with no specific place for the counter, on the other hand, implies that it should be accepted.

9. Know When to Stop Countering. Sometimes you and the sellers are so far off on price or terms that it becomes obvious that there is no real room for compromise. For example, the best offer you can make is $212,000 and the best counter the seller can make is $250,000. Sometimes you may have to accept the fact that not all deals can be made.

Refusing to counter can also be a bargaining tool. After several counteroffers you're still apart on price or terms. Instead of accepting the sellers' most recent counter, you do a "walkaway" and send it back. You include a signed statement to the effect that your last counteroffer (the one before the sellers made their most recent counter) is your final and best offer.

You'll give the sellers until midnight to accept it or you're no longer interested in the property.

Further, you're not interested in any more counteroffers from the sellers.

The idea here is to decide the deal on a single throw of the dice. It's all or nothing. You're tired of bargaining. Either the sellers accept what you've offered or you'll go elsewhere. You're wagering all on one toss of the dice.

I've personally used this technique many times and it works for me more often than it fails! You just have to be prepared to give up the house in case the sellers remain adamant.

Be Sure Your Agent Wants to Make Your Offer

Some agents simply refuse to take a lowball offer. They may say something like, "I can't take this offer to the seller. You'll just have to offer more."

Baloney. A seller's agent has to take every legitimate offer to the seller. A legitimate offer is one that is in writing with a deposit. Your agent may not like it, but he or she will do it. On the other hand, if the agent is reticent to submit the offer, you'd do better by finding a different agent who is more willing to try to get your price accepted.

By the way, if you are using a buyer's agent (as described in Chapter 4), it is incumbent on that agent to get for you the best price the seller is likely to accept. You can rely much more heavily on a buyer's agent's advice than on a seller's agent's or a dual agent's comments.

Tricks of the Trade

Here are some suggestions, a few surprising, that you may want to try. They could help you to get a better deal.

Have You Asked the Sellers What Their Lowest Price Is?

This may come as a surprise to many buyers. "You mean I can talk to the seller?" Of course you can. The worst the seller can say is, "I'm not discussing the sale. Talk to my agent." The best the seller can do is to tell you how desperate he or she is and how urgently a sale is needed—and how low an offer might be accepted.

Don't Let Your Agent Distract You

Your agent isn't likely to encourage you to talk to the seller. That bypasses the agent and arouses all kinds of suspicions (like maybe you're trying to finagle a deal to avoid paying a commission). Don't worry. They won't put you behind bars for talking to the seller. Just remember, the seller is only a phone call away.

On the other hand, don't try to bypass the agent to avoid the commission—even though a seller may suggest this, offering to split the cost of the commission through a lower price. You probably won't succeed (the seller is undoubtedly tied up by a listing agreement) and you'll only offend your agent, whom you want to be on your side.

Keep in mind that most listing agreements provide that a commission must be paid to an agent for months after the listing expires if the buyer (you) was shown the house during the listing period by the agent.

You would have to wait months in order for this finagling to be effective, and during that time chances are that someone else would come along and buy the property out from under you.

Have You Tried an "Appraisal Offer"?

If the sellers seem adamant and won't budge on the price, a daring approach is to make an offer with the price contingent upon an appraisal. In other words, you'll agree to accept whatever the appraiser says the property is worth if the sellers will likewise accept it. (Usually there are "outs" included which provide that if the price is above a certain point, you won't accept or if it's below a certain point, the seller doesn't have to go through with it.)

An offer contingent on appraisal is sometimes done with investment properties, but rarely with houses. Nevertheless, if you have a seller who's convinced that the sales price is right and won't budge, it's another alternative. Just be sure that you agree in advance on who the appraiser is and who is to pay the appraisal fee.

On the other hand, the trouble with hiring an appraiser is that it usually takes too much time and is too expensive (typically $250 to $450). But if you have the time and want a professionally acquired figure for the true market value of the property, you can call in an appraiser. And if the appraisal comes in low, it can provide ammunition to blast the seller down from a high asking price.

The All Important Purchase Agreement

We all instinctively know that no deal is done until the paperwork is done. Real estate, however, asks a bit more. Here, no deal is even begun until the paperwork is done. Indeed, according to the Statute of Frauds, all agreements for the purchase of real property *must* be in writing. The paperwork, therefore, is critical to making the deal.

In this chapter we'll look at the purchase agreement, the document you'll use to make your offer. And the document that's also used to counteroffer, when your original offer isn't accepted.

First, however, let's make sure we understand the 10 steps involved in purchasing your home and where the paperwork fits in.

The 10 Steps to Making a Purchase

1. Get preapproved
2. Find and work with an agent

3. Locate the right home
4. Make an offer (on a purchase agreement)
5. Counteroffer (on a purchase agreement)
6. Open escrow (sign escrow instructions)
7. Secure your financing (get estimated cost documents from lender)
8. Remove contingencies (documents prepared in escrow)
9. Have a final walk-through
10. Sign and take possession (sign the loan docs and other papers)

The *Official* Offer Starts with the Purchase Agreement

The whole process of buying a home is defined by the purchase agreement (also sometimes called the "sales offer" or "deposit receipt"). It's the governing document of the transaction. After it's accepted, it determines how the rest of the sale is handled, what you get, for how much money, and on what terms.

How We Got to Today's Purchase Agreements

In the old days in real estate the sales agreement was usually just one page long. It had very little printed material and was composed mostly of empty spaces that the agent filled out. That has changed dramatically.

Over the years dissatisfied buyers and sellers (a small minority, but with important implications) have gone to court, fighting over various issues such as contingencies, deposits, and damages. What they discovered was that the sales agreement, drawn up not by an attorney but by a real estate agent, might not hold up. In fact, in some cases the agreement was completely defective.

This resulted in additional suits, sometimes against agents, almost all of whom now carry a form of malpractice or errors and omissions insurance.

It also resulted in a new kind of sales agreement. The new agreement is created by attorneys and is frequently many (read 10 or more) pages long. Almost all of it is printed out—the agent typically only checks boxes or fills in dollar amounts.

In fact, there are very few places that the agent (or you) even has the opportunity to write anything new. The whole emphasis is on seeing to it that relatively little can be added or changed for fear that it may void or weaken the agreement.

TIP

Because the sales agreement is intended to be a legally binding document, you should have your real estate attorney check it over and explain the full ramifications of it to you, and advise you, before you sign it.

In addition to legal considerations, which you should pursue with your attorney, there are important practical issues in the purchase agreement that involve the kind of a deal you're going to get. These typically include the following areas. (If yours does not cover these areas, you should ask your agent or attorney why it does not.)

Practical Areas Your Purchase Agreement Should Cover

- Price, down payment, and deposit
- Specific terms for all financing
- Street improvements or bonds (if any, who pays for them)
- When you will be given occupancy
- How long the seller has to accept the offer
- The term of the escrow (how long it will be open)
- How you will take title (tenants in common, joint tenancy, community property, and so on; see your lawyer, since

there are important tax and legal ramifications for how you take title)

- Liquidated damages and arbitration in case of disputes
- Any personal property involved
- Foreign tax withholding (applies if the seller is a foreigner)
- When and how the seller will give you a disclosure statement about the property
- Seller's warranties
- When and how you'll be able to conduct a professional inspection
- When and how a termite report will be issued
- If soil, geological, or other tests are required, how they will be conducted
- If there are concerns about flood or water hazards (noting if the property is in any flood hazard area), how they will be carried out and what form they will take
- Other disclosures, such as zoning problems (indicating if the property is in a special zone, such as a "coastal zone," which could affect your ability to build or add on)
- If you get a Home Protection Plan (which pays for damage or problems with the heating, plumbing, electrical, and other systems), who pays for it
- Energy retrofit disclosure procedures (local or state ordinances sometimes require additional items such as insulation to be placed in the house when the property is sold)
- How prorations will be handled
- Other contingencies and areas involved in the sale

Many of the areas covered by the sales agreement, such as price, are obvious. Others are discussed in different sections of this book. Now, however, we're going to look at some selected areas of a typical sales agreement that usually are of particular interest to buyers.

Remember, for advice consult a professional such as your attorney or agent.

How Big a Deposit Should You Put Up?

Once you've settled on the price, the next consideration for most buyers is the deposit. The deposit is money that you put up at the time you make an offer on a piece of property to show that you are in earnest about buying it. (You're putting your money where your mouth is, so to speak.) Hence the deposit is actually "earnest money." It is supposed to demonstrate to the seller that your offer isn't capricious.

An offer can be made without a deposit. However, a seller is less likely to accept it. After all, without a deposit you have very little to lose by not following through on the deal.

Some agents will insist that you put up a big deposit. They argue that this will help convince the seller to accept your offer. While there is a germ of truth here, there is also a lot of chaff, as we'll see shortly. You can offer any amount as a deposit.

TRAP

Today, a good agent may suggest you simply put up $1,000 to $10,000 "to make the offer official." Of course, that same agent may insist that you be willing to increase that offer substantially once all contingencies have been removed.

Agents often suggest that you offer 5 percent of the purchase price. On a $100,000 property that's $5,000. But on a $500,000 property, it's $25,000.

To my thinking, in today's market any initial deposit of more than $5,000, or $10,000 for a very expensive home, is a waste. You're simply putting your money unnecessarily at risk. The reason is that, unlike in the past, today's deals hinge on all sorts of contingencies. For example, the deal is rarely solid until you've approved a professional inspection and the seller's disclosures. If these contingencies aren't removed, the deal doesn't go forward and your deposit is normally returned.

Thus, a large deposit today doesn't mean what it used to. It won't impress the seller's agent. And it won't impress a sharp seller. (They would be more impressed by a solid preapproval letter from a lender.)

TIP

No matter how likely it is that your deposit will be returned, any money you put up is at risk. Therefore, it's to your advantage to put as little at risk as possible. Remember, you can agree to add to the deposit later, after the seller and you have removed the contingencies.

Sellers may demand in the purchase agreement that once the offer has been accepted and you've had a chance to inspect and approve the property and disclosures (and, perhaps once financing has been arranged), you will put up an additional amount of money in the deposit. This could be a substantial increase.

Increasing the deposit has two important effects. It assures the seller that you are serious (in earnest) about completing the transaction. And second, it means that you might lose your deposit, since you've already cleared the contingencies which might otherwise allow you to gracefully get it back.

You won't want to increase your deposit unless and until you're sure you're going to want to and be able to go through with the purchase. On the other hand, refusing to increase your deposit, as agreed to in the purchase offer, could nix the deal.

Must a Deposit Be in Cash?

A deposit doesn't necessarily have to be in the form of cash. It can be a promissory note or a check that all parties agree not to cash or even personal property such as the title to a car or boat. Cash (cashier's check), however, talks the loudest when you're trying to convince a seller to accept an offer.

Sometimes sellers will specify in a listing agreement that they will accept no offers with less than, for example, a $5,000 cash deposit. Remember, however, everything is negotiable. You can always offer a smaller deposit in a different form.

However, if the seller is demanding a $5,000 cash deposit, the agent may not be required to submit lesser offers, depending on how the listing agreement was signed.

Most agents, however, will submit any and all offers.

Will You Get Your Deposit Back?

At this point, I'm sure some readers are wondering, "What's the big deal, anyway? Why not put up a bigger deposit?" Too often buyers simply put their faith in their agent and the purchase agreement and assume that everything is bound to turn out okay. If the deal sours, they'll get their money back.

In most cases, this in fact is the way it does turn out. But, not always. Sometimes when things go bad, they can go bad very quickly and very badly, particularly in terms of the deposit.

There are at least two problem areas you should know about: (1) Who holds the deposit? and (2) How do you get it back if the deal falls through?

Who Holds the Deposit?

The seller is entitled to the deposit. However, the seller is the last person in the world you want to give the deposit to. The seller might immediately spend the money, then later on, if the deal falls through, might not be able to refund it to you, even if you're entitled to get it back. It could require the services of an attorney and a lawsuit to secure the return of the deposit from the seller and that could be very costly. In other words, giving the deposit to the seller could be like dropping it down a deep hole.

You want the deposit to go to a neutral third party who will not frivolously spend the money, but who will hold it and have it on hand to pay you back, if necessary. The first most likely candidate here might be the agent. Possibly the next best candidate may be an escrow company, though not necessarily (see below).

Should You Give Your Deposit to Your Agent? Real estate agents are required to maintain trust accounts for any money they receive. In other words, they can't commingle (mix) your money with their own, but must hold it in a separate account in trust for you. This is to keep them from spending your money. While that sounds safe, the problem is that, in theory, the deposit belongs to the seller and if the seller demands it, the seller's agent is supposed to hand the deposit over. Most agents, however, are as wary of the seller as you are and will do everything possible to hold the money in trust until the deal closes.

TIP

Agents must normally hold your money in a special fiduciary account. In many states the most common reason for real estate license suspension or revocation is the commingling (mixing) of the agent's funds with yours. It's not that agents are all that dishonest; it's that sometimes they are lousy accountants.

To ensure that they don't lose their licenses, agents almost always will bend over backward to repay any money stuck in their trust accounts. Further, many states have special recovery funds. If you lose money through the carelessness (or fraud) of an agent, you may be able to recover it from the state, even though it could take years. Check with your state's department of real estate.

Should You Give Your Deposit to an Escrow Company?   Today, many good agents realize that accepting a check for a deposit puts them at great risk. If the deal doesn't go through, both the buyer and the seller may demand the money, leaving the agent in the middle. To avoid this, many agents suggest you write the deposit check out to an escrow company, which, you agree in advance, will handle the escrow of the property if and when the seller accepts. In other words, give the deposit to a neutral party. Sound good?

There is also peril here. If, after the seller accepts, the deal still falls apart, even through no fault of your own, it might be hard to get the deposit back even from a neutral escrow.

The reason is that escrows simply handle the documents and funds in a transaction. In order for an escrow to operate, both buyer *and* seller must agree to the escrow's instructions. If, for example, you tell the escrow to return your money and the seller tells the escrow to hold onto it, there's no agreement. And your money remains in limbo. This affects you more than the seller. After all, it's your money.

Sometimes in this situation sellers are content to let the money sit in an inactive escrow for months just to "punish" a buyer for a deal that falls through. Fortunately, calmer minds usually prevail and sellers eventually will agree to release your funds, once they become convinced that there's no way they can get the money and that to continue to hold it might result in a lawsuit against them.

TIP

Making your check payable to an escrow does ensure that it goes to a neutral third party. It does not, however, guarantee that you'll get it back quickly, easily, or at all.

What If the Deal Falls Through?

What must be obvious by now is that putting up a deposit is a sometimes tricky thing that can have significant consequences. How do you get the deposit back, for example, if the deal doesn't go through?

There are at least two considerations here: First, why didn't the deal go through? If it's your fault, you may not be entitled to a return of the deposit. Second, if you are entitled to a return, how do you get the funds transferred back to you?

Operating on the principle that the time to consult an attorney is before you need one, I advise you to seek the services of a professional real estate lawyer at this juncture. Chances are you're going to need one anyway before the deal is concluded, and by bringing the lawyer in at an early stage, you could avoid much grief.

(Most lawyers who deal in real estate have set fees that are much lower than for general legal work. Ask the lawyer in advance what the fees are.)

What If the Seller Doesn't Accept Your Offer?   That's easy, or should be. If the seller does not accept your offer, you're entitled to your deposit back, immediately. It's just that simple.

The seller has to agree to your entire offer, including any terms you propose. If the seller agrees to the price but not the terms and counters with different terms, which you don't accept, there's no deal and you're entitled to your money back. If the seller accepts your terms but counters with a different price, which you don't accept, the deal is off and you're entitled to your deposit back.

The moment the seller declines your offer and "counters" (proposes a deal different in some way, no matter how small), the original offer is dead. Unless you accept the seller's counteroffer, you're entitled to your deposit back.

Once in a very great while an unscrupulous agent will say something such as, "Even though the seller didn't accept, I made a good-faith effort to get the deal through. Therefore, I'm entitled to half the deposit. I'll return half to you and keep the other half." (Most listings specify that the agent and the seller will split any forfeit deposits.)

No way. If the deal was never made, if the loss of the deal wasn't your fault, if the seller isn't allowed to keep the deposit, the agent doesn't get a part of it either. (Note: If you sign an agreement with a buyer's agent, be sure to read it carefully, especially with regard to how the deposit is handled.)

What If the Seller Accepts and Then, Later On, the Deal Falls Through because of You? There are many reasons the deal might fall through because of you. For example, you could be counting on Aunt Harriet to give you the money for the down payment. You get the seller to sign an offer, secure financing, and poor Aunt Harriet has a heart attack and dies. Her money will be tied up in probate for years.

Sure, you didn't do anything intentionally to quash the deal, but you don't have the expected money to perform. As far as the seller is concerned, it's your fault.

Or you get cold feet. You take a look at those huge monthly payments and you decide that you can't go through with it. You want out, period.

Or you find another house that is really perfect. You want to get out of this deal so that you can get the other.

Or . . . There are lots of reasons that you might not want or be able to perform on your end of a purchase agreement. The point here is, however, that for whatever reason, if it's your fault the deal doesn't go forward and if you don't have a contingency clause protecting you (see below), your chances of getting the deposit back are not good.

In fact, you could be in hot water and liable for a lot more than just the deposit. The seller could decide to sue you for specific performance demanding that you complete the transaction, or pay damages.

Most sales agreements provide that if you default, the seller is entitled to keep the deposit. Thus, at least in theory, if you default on the deal, your deposit is lost. And, of course, there could be an irate seller to deal with.

Of course, it could all be litigated at great expense, exasperation, and cost.

In the past when a buyer defaulted, a seller occasionally did sue to both keep the deposit and for damages, thus tying up the courts and causing long-term problems for everyone concerned. As a result, liquidated-damage clauses for residential real estate have come into wide use in sales agreements and are accepted and even codified in many states.

Will a "Liquidated Damages" Clause Protect You?

Basically these clauses state that if you and the seller agree in advance, the deposit (or a portion of it) will constitute the entire damages the seller is entitled to in the event of your default. In other words, if the deal doesn't go through and it's clearly your fault, you agree in advance that the seller can keep the deposit, provided she or he agrees not to sue you for additional damages or specific performance.

Many states put limitations on liquidated damages. For practical purposes, the seller is usually satisfied with them, and unless you're litigious by nature, you probably are satisfied too.

You may be asked to sign or initial a liquidated damage clause in the sales agreement that states that if you do not go through with the sale, your deposit is automatically forfeited in exchange for the seller's not suing you for specific performance. Should you sign?

Ask your attorney. On the one hand, signing the clause (assuming the seller also signs) may help to limit your loss in the event of your default to the deposit receipt. On the other hand, it almost ensures that you'll lose the entire deposit, whereas, depending on the situation, you might otherwise get at least a portion back.

Goodwill Often Plays a Role

While what potentially can or cannot happen may seem quite dire, what actually happens in practice if a deal collapses can be benign. On the one hand, if you simply back out because you change your mind or find a better house, chances are that neither the seller's agent nor the seller is going to be sympathetic and you stand an excellent chance of having them demand your deposit.

On the other hand, if circumstances cause you to default—your aunt, whom you were counting on for money, dies or you get sick or injured or something happens that is truly beyond your control—then it's often a different story. Here, you are truly relying on the goodwill of the seller's agent and the seller. In most cases I have seen of this kind of occurrence, the buyer has gotten most, if not all, of the deposit back.

Agents are not in the business to make money on deposits. Sellers are interested in selling, not in keeping the deposit of a person who falls on hard times. I have seen agents bend over backward in these circumstances to get the seller to give the deposit back. I have seen sellers gladly return the deposit, sometimes over the agent's objections. Of course, you could get the bad apples, but goodwill in people is everywhere.

What If the Seller (Not You) Fails to Go Through with the Deal?

Why would a seller fail to go through with a deal, once signed?

Simple. You offer $250,000 for a house and the seller accepts. Two days later another buyer comes in with an offer of $300,000. Wouldn't it be wonderful if the seller could get out of your deal and accept the new one? The seller would stand to make an additional $50,000. That's plenty of reason to default.

In these circumstances you are fully justified in demanding the return of your deposit. In addition, you may want to sue the seller for specific performance, to force a sale to you. (After all, you could then resell for the higher price and keep the profit yourself!)

When the seller defaults, you usually will get the deposit back. Typically the seller is more than happy to do everything necessary to get that deposit back to you in the hope that you won't take further action.

If you still want the property, check with your attorney. You may decide to take further action.

What If It's No One's Fault, but the Deal Just Can't Be Made?

There are a lot of reasons that a deal might not go through. You may not be able to secure adequate financing. The title to the property may not be clear. There could be extensive termite damage. The reasons are endless and they crop up in a good many deals.

In most cases there's a way to work them out: Other financing is secured. The seller clears the title. The termite damage is fixed. And so on. In other words, the problems are solved one way or another.

However, sometimes it just doesn't work out and there's no deal to be made. What happens to your deposit then?

If you've given it to an agent who has kept it in a personal trust account, you can demand it back and in most cases the agent will immediately return it (perhaps risking the ire of the seller). If the conditions of the purchase agreement can't be fulfilled, normally you're entitled to get the deposit back and most agents don't want to argue the point.

On the other hand, if the deposit's been placed in an escrow account, it takes both the buyer's and the seller's agreement to get it out.

Maybe the seller is angry that the deal fell through and says, "I'm not signing anything." There your deposit sits, even though you're perfectly entitled to it. Unless the agent can prevail and convince the seller to release it, it could remain there for a long time!

As a practical matter, however, as soon as another buyer comes along, the seller probably will be forced to release it so as not to jeopardize a later sale.

All of which brings us back to my original point. The money you put up for deposit is at risk. The less you put up, the less you risk.

What Are "Contingencies"?

A contingency clause is essentially any clause in a contract that says the offer depends or hinges on some other event or action. For example, wording that would say "This offer is contingent upon the buyer's winning the state lottery" is a kind of contingency clause, a frivolous one that obviously no sane seller would accept.

I once knew a builder whose advice was, "No matter what the contract, always be sure that somewhere in it, it says, 'subject to.' I don't care what comes after the 'subject to,' just as long as it's in there." The words "subject to" have essentially the same meaning as "contingent." They make the sales offer hinge on some event or action. What my builder friend meant was that as long as those words were in it, he could get out of the contract if he had to. He had many experiences fighting subcontractors, landowners, and others, and I firmly believe to this day that he could get out of any contract with those words in it. For your purposes, however, a contingency clause is very useful to protect you against an unforeseen change of condition.

Some contingencies are absolutely necessary in the sales agreement for the protection of the buyer, and few agents would hesitate to put them in. Typical contingency clauses include:

Common Contingency Clauses

- **Financing.** If you can't get the financing you need, there is no deal and you get your deposit back.
- **Disclosures.** You have the right to approve the seller's property disclosures. Don't approve them and there's no deal.
- **Professional inspection.** You have the right to approve a professional inspection report. Don't approve it and the deal's off.

Of course, there may be some other contingency that you need added to the deal.

TRAP

The more you protect yourself with contingencies, the less the seller is going to want to sign your offer. After all, if you make it full of contingencies, it's like Swiss cheese, it holds little water and you could slip out of the deal at your pleasure.

What About a Pending Sale Contingency?

Here you make your offer contingent on the sale of your current home which is already in escrow. If your current home falls out of escrow, then you're not committed to move forward with the new deal. You could also make the sale of your new home contingent, even if you haven't yet found a buyer for your old one.

In a cold market, sometimes sellers who are desperate will accept this contingency. In a good market, however, most won't. They realize they are tying the sale of their house to the sale of someone else's house. It's like having to make two deals instead of one.

What About a Frivolous Contingency?

As noted, you can make the deal contingent on almost anything from the occurrence of sunspots to your winning the Irish Sweepstakes. However, don't expect a seller to be thrilled about these. The more frivolous your contingencies appear, the less likely you are to get the seller to accept your offer.

Who Should Write the Contingency?

Most modern purchase agreements have the most common contingencies already written in. Your agent simply checks the appropriate box and the contingency is in effect. Of course, you may want to have your attorney check the language used in the agreement just to be sure.

If a new contingency is to be written, it should be handled by an attorney. This does not mean that a good agent can't do it. Many agents with years of experience can handle these easily. Even so, it wouldn't hurt to have an attorney recheck it, just to be sure.

What Terms Should You Offer?

The terms of a purchase can sometimes be more important than the price. (Terms are often structured in the form of a contingency, see above.)

Sellers are often hung up on price. Offer them their full price and they may give you ridiculously favorable terms. For example, to get their price, the sellers just might be willing to finance the sale (carry back a mortgage). If you're having credit problems, it's something to consider.

What Are Time Terms?

There are other terms you might consider. One of the most crucial is time. How long do you have to secure financing, to come up with the down payment and closing costs, to close the escrow?

Time is often negotiated. Perhaps the seller wants 90 days before moving out. That suits you fine, so there is immediate agreement.

On the other hand, perhaps the seller wants to close escrow in 30 days, but you feel you'll need 90 to raise the cash for the down payment.

Now time is a negotiating point. You compromise. You'll take a chance on coming up with the cash in 60 days, but the seller has to be willing to lower the price $5,000, or throw in the refrigerator and that beautiful chandelier.

The seller balks and says the most he can go is 45 days, but he'll lower the interest rate on the second mortgage he's carrying from 9 percent to 8 percent and throw in the refrigerator. Is it okay with you?

Now you have to make a judgment call. The agent may suggest a "bridge" loan (temporary financing until you can get your cash) to cover the extra time you'll need. But this costs you extra money.

In the final analysis, you'll have to weigh all the factors regarding time. Just remember it's a negotiating card, one which you can play.

What Are Other Terms?

There are a host of other common terms in a real estate transaction, almost all of which are negotiable. For example, you may agree to pay full price for a property *if* the seller agrees to pay your closing costs.

Or you'll buy only if the seller agrees to pay for a special mold and mildew inspection (offered by some termite and fungus infestation removal companies) as well as any repair work removing black mold.

Or . . .?

Unfortunately, throughout all of this bargaining you're going to have to pretty much rely on yourself. Certainly your agent will be there to try and protect you. However, if you want some particularly onerous terms (to the seller), your agent might not be too happy, as it could make it harder to get the seller to sign. And I've never met an agent who wanted to work harder closing a deal.

Thus, it's up to you to get the best terms.

As noted earlier, the time to consult an attorney is before you need one. At this juncture a real estate attorney can prove extremely useful. The attorney can create a purchase agreement that protects you as well as writing in the most favorable terms (for you).

TRAP

Beware of attorneys who work too hard for your interests. In general, real estate agents dread attorneys, not because they aren't competent or because they don't protect people, but because they tend to muck up deals. There's an old saying among real estate agents that the fastest way to have a deal go sour is to bring in an attorney. Yes, you want your rights protected and you want the most favorable terms. But you also want to ultimately purchase the house. An attorney can create a sales contract so favorable to you that no seller will accept it. As with the ancient Greeks, moderation is in order. Allow your attorney to draw up the terms correctly and to advise. But also rely on common sense.

When Do You Get Possession?

The question here is: When will you take possession of the property? The most common answer is: at the close of escrow after title has been recorded in your name.

The danger with occupancy is that the sellers won't move out. There are many reasons the sellers might not move. A new house they are planning to move into might not be ready. Or there might be illness in the family and a family member might not be easily moved. Or they could just be ornery.

Whatever the reason, if they don't move, it spells trouble for you. If the sellers are still in possession of the house once you get title, you can't easily have them removed. (In the old days "self-help eviction" was allowed—you could physically go in and throw them out! That's been a taboo for quite a few decades now.)

To get the sellers out you might need to conduct an "unlawful detainer" action through the courts—eviction. This usually takes at least a month, may cost upwards of $2,000 or more, and usually requires the services of an attorney.

TIP

There's an easy way to help ensure that there is no problem with occupancy. Be sure that the purchase agreement specifies (in a contingency) that the sellers are to be out by the time escrow closes, preferably at least one day in advance of the close. Then, before signing all the closing documents that buyers usually sign, check to see that the sellers have complied. If the property is empty, it's a good sign that the sellers are out, and you're free to sign. If they're not out, it could be a problem, and you may not want to sign—check with your agent and attorney.

On the other hand, there are extenuating circumstances. You may want to move in early to get your kids registered in school. The sellers may want to move out late, so their kids don't have to switch schools midterm.

In these situations, a rental agreement might be arranged. If you move in early (assuming the property is already empty), you pay the sellers rent. If they stay late, they pay you rent.

TRAP

Tenant agreements can lead to trouble. Let's say the sellers want to stay after the close of escrow, after ownership transfers to you. They then become tenants, with all the rights that tenants have. They might not later move as agreed. They might leave the property a mess. You can somewhat reduce these problems by having the sellers sign a strong tenant's agreement, along with rent sufficient to make your monthly payment, and a hefty security deposit to cover breakage and cleaning. However, if they refuse to move as agreed, you might still need to have them evicted.

Should You Insist on a Final Walk-Through?

You see the property before you make the offer. The offer's made and accepted. Then there's a wait of a month or so while financing is arranged, title is cleared, and so forth. Now you're ready to close the deal. But, how do you know that now the property is in the same condition as when you first saw it? How do you know the seller hasn't smashed holes in the walls and broken the appliances? (Unlikely, but it does happen.) How do you know there aren't scratches on the floor, damaged sinks and toilets, and so on?

You know by insisting the purchase agreement give you the right to a final walk-through inspection. Before the deal closes, you once again examine what you are buying to be sure it's as you first saw it (or reasonably close).

It's important to understand that a final walk-through is not supposed to be an opportunity for you to reconsider your purchase or reopen negotiations. It is just supposed to be a chance for you to examine the property to see that it's as it was when you originally made your offer. Most savvy sellers will include a clause stating if something of consequence is found wrong, the sellers have the right to correct it—that the final walk-through is not intended to be a new beginning in negotiating price or terms.

Nonetheless, buyers have used faults found on the final inspection to attempt to back out of a deal at the last minute. (Their reasons can vary from finding a serious fault in the property to finding another more preferable house.) My suggestion is that if you want to renegotiate based on the final walk-though, you better have found some serious problem with the house, else you'll have an angry seller to contend with.

Sometimes agents will suggest that a specific date for the final walk-through be written into the purchase agreement. I feel this is usually a bad idea. You don't want to set a specific date because you don't know when escrow will close and you'll get occupancy. I prefer that the final inspection should be set as close to the day escrow closes as possible, preferably a day or two before.

Keep in mind that if you inspect the property too early, the sellers may still be living in it and furniture and carpets not yet removed may conceal potential damage. Try to be sure the sellers are out before you have your final inspection. (This also helps solve the problem of occupancy noted above.)

TIP

Be sure the gas, electricity, and water are on when you have your "walk-through" inspection. Otherwise, you won't be able to tell if any of the house's systems are broken.

Expect Dirt and Minor Damage

Don't expect the property to look as clean as it did when you first saw it. If the seller was living in the property when you first saw it, carpets and furniture hid a lot of marks and scuffing. Once the furniture and carpeting are removed these stand out like sore thumbs.

Dark scratch marks on walls and scrapes on floors are common. Indentations in carpeting where heavy furniture stood are also common, as is some slight discoloration. (This carpet indentation will usually disappear within a few days on its own, but not always.)

What you need to look for is any significant breakage, damage, or other condition that was not there when you first saw the home, or when you had your professional home inspection. Also, check for any damaged or broken item that the seller did not disclose in the sales agreement or accompanying documents.

What specifically should you look for?

Items to Watch Out For in a Final Walk-Through

- Holes in wall, broken plaster
- Broken windows
- Inoperative or broken appliances such as stove, garbage disposal, and oven
- Faulty or broken water heater (as evidenced by no hot water), gas heater, or air conditioner. Check to see that the heater heats and the air conditioner cools.
- Gashes, slashes, or marks in wood floors that will require redoing the floor
- Damaged or inoperative light fixtures
- Broken or inoperative heating or air-conditioning thermostat
- Leaky or inoperative plumbing, as evidenced by new water marks or water on floors
- Defects in the electrical system, often evidenced by light switches or wall plugs that don't work
- New damage to carpet, such as dirt or, most important, cat or dog urination. I've seen sellers who let their pets run loose in the house after the sales agreement was signed, figuring that it wasn't their problem any more. But if you accept a carpet that has been ruined by urination, it's a big

problem for you. Odor is usually the giveaway. If you sus-
pect a problem, don't hesitate to get down on your hands
and knees to check it out. Better to discover it now than
when you're the owner.

- Any other damage or change in the home's condition

TRAP

I have found that urine stains from pets *cannot* be effectively removed from carpeting. Typically the carpeting and usually the pad underneath (and sometimes
even the flooring!) must be replaced. An entire house's carpeting might need to be
replaced to match a small area of damage. I won't accept a carpet problem
caused by pets. Insist it be fixed, even if that requires the sellers to recarpet the
entire house. (Be sure you approve the quality of carpeting and padding they use.)

What About a Professional Home Inspection?

Yes, you should have it for your own protection. Just remember
that in most cases, the buyer pays for the inspection and it costs
around $300. But it may very well turn out to be money well
spent. Also check into Chapter 16.

Should You Insist on a Home Protection Plan?

Several national companies offer plans which give you some insurance protection for the major systems of your home. Typically
they cover plumbing (including water heater), heating, air-conditioning, electrical, appliances, and so forth. The idea is that for a
set period of time after you move in (usually one year), should
there be a problem, the home protection company will cover it.
The cost is usually nominal, a few hundred dollars for a year's
worth of coverage.

In most purchases the sellers pay for the plan; you pay the
deductible (usually under $50) for each time you call someone out

to deal with a problem. Most plans are renewable, so if you like the one you've got, you can keep it. (Of course, you'll have to pay for it yourself after the first year!)

The home protection plan should be included as part of the purchase agreement. The agreement should state that it will be purchased at the time of sale, and that the seller will provide the appropriate warranties. (The seller is usually required to warrant that everything is in working condition before the plan takes effect.) If you wait until after title transfers, you either may not be able to get the plan or may find that *you* have to warrant the condition of the various home systems only to discover that some aren't working!

Should You Agree to an Arbitration Clause?

Some sales agreements contain arbitration clauses. Typically these refer only to the deposit, but in some cases they may refer to other areas. Basically what they say is that if there is a disagreement, you will submit it to binding arbitration—you will go along with whatever an arbitrator says.

Keep in mind that you could be giving up significant rights if you sign an arbitration agreement. If the seller refuses to go through with the deal after you've made all sorts of commitments (from accepting a new job to putting your kids in a new school to moving across the country), you're likely to be quite upset. You might want the right to sue for damages.

However, you could lose the option of suing the seller for damages or specific performance (forcing them to sell to you) by signing this clause. (On the other hand, the seller could be giving up the same rights, meaning that you could be avoiding the risk of being sued.) It's a good idea to ask your attorney about this clause.

If you agree to arbitration, just remember that for it to be effective both you (the buyer) and the seller have to agree. If just one agrees, it won't work.

Also, be sure you know who the arbitrator will be. Many arbitration clauses specify that the arbitrator will be a member of the American Arbitration Association (local members are listed in the yellow pages of your phone book). This is fine, since such members are skilled at arbitration. But they are also quite expensive. It really doesn't make much sense to use an arbitrator when his or her fee may exceed the worth of the item being arbitrated.

Do You Understand "Prorations"?

Typically there are always some items that are "prorated" such as taxes, fire insurance, or interest on a mortgage you might be assuming. This means they are adjusted based on who owes them.

For example, a fire insurance policy is typically written and paid for at least one year in advance. However, the house may be sold after the policy has been in effect for only three months. You, the buyer, may be taking over the policy. In this case the seller will undoubtedly want to "prorate" the cost of the insurance policy. In other words, you would pay the seller back for the nine unused months you are going to be using the policy.

The same applies to prepaid taxes or taxes that are owing. Adjustments are made in your favor or the seller's favor, depending on when payment was made and what the date of proration is.

There are only two questions with regard to proration: What will be prorated and on what date? Typically all items that are affected by time are prorated. Usually the proration date is the close of escrow.

Should You Write In Personal Property That Goes with the Sale?

When you purchase a home, you are basically buying "real property." Loosely defined, real property is the land, the house, and anything that's permanently attached to it. For example, the windows in the house are real property.

Personal property, on the other hand, is everything else. Furniture is personal property, as are dishes, clothes, and most things that you can take with you.

For most things the definition of what's personal and what's real property is easily grasped and readily agreed to. However, in some circumstances the line between personal and real becomes gray and that's when you can run into trouble.

For example, wall-to-wall carpeting that is tacked down is normally considered real property—it's permanently attached to the house. But what about a rug that is thrown over the floor and not attached? Normally, it would be considered personal property.

Drapes that are hung on rods are usually considered personal property if you can take them off without in any way damaging the house. But the rods that hold the drapes and that are affixed by screws into the walls of the house may be considered real property.

Can you see where problems could arise? You see a house and you fall in love with it. It is completely carpeted with throw rugs and drapes. You buy it. But on your final walk-through, all the carpeting is gone, as are the drapes. What happened?

"Why," the seller remarks innocently, "those were my personal property and I took them along with the furniture." Is the seller allowed to do that? Probably, if the items weren't permanently attached and if no mention of them was made in the sales agreement.

Don't assume anything when it comes to items such as rugs, drapes, and even appliances. (Yes, appliances! Most so-called built-in stoves and ovens just pull out and unplug. Unless they are included in a sales agreement, a seller may feel they are personal property too!) Assume they are personal property unless you are specifically told they are not.

It is because of the confusion between personal and real property that today most sales agreements include a clause which states that all appliances, wall coverings, and floor coverings are included with the purchase, "except_____" and a space is left to write in any exceptions. A separate clause may include all appliances and light fixtures. Look for these clauses in the sales agreement, and if they are not there, ask your agent and/or attorney why they are not.

TIP

Sometimes you can take advantage of these in between areas between real and personal property. For example, you look at a house and you are impressed with the kitchen. It has had a makeover and is truly beautiful. There are impressive oak cabinets and a special wall cabinet into which a large two-door refrigerator fits perfectly. You ask about the refrigerator and are told that it, of course, is the personal property of the sellers. It's not included in the sale. But, you think to yourself, where in the world am I ever going to find another refrigerator to fit so perfectly in there? Isn't it a shame that it doesn't go with the house? Well, of course, you can make it go with the house. When you write up your offer to purchase, indicate that one of the conditions of sale (a contingency) is that the refrigerator goes with the house. No refrigerator, no deal. Will the sellers accept? It depends on how anxious they are to sell. If you're the first serious buyer to come along in months, they'll probably grab it.

Pay Careful Attention to Your Purchase Agreement

The purchase agreement is where you make your deal (good, bad, or mediocre) and define how the purchase process will be followed until the house is yours. Take time with the sales agreement and make sure that you understand it thoroughly. Check with your agent and attorney. Be sure you're getting all that you can. Be sure you're writing up the best deal possible.

Closing the Deal

You've found a house, negotiated with the seller, signed a purchase agreement, and now you're home free. Right?

Almost. But, you still have to close the deal. Escrow (an independent third party, usually a company, but sometimes an attorney) will be opened. The actual purchase of real estate takes time, typically 30 to 45 days. During that time you'll have to complete the details of financing with your lender, and the seller will have to prepare the property and clear title. (You'll be asked to sign preliminary escrow instructions that reflect the purchase agreement and tell the escrow agent what needs to be done to close the deal.)

The closing is a critical period. And it all ends one day when escrow is complete or "perfect"—everything required to close the transaction has been done. At that time you're usually asked into the escrow company and are required to sign sheaves of paper and give out numerous checks. After that, the deed and loan documents are recorded and the home becomes yours.

For the newcomer to real estate transactions, the signing can be a real surprise, particularly when it comes to the costs. They can be many thousands of dollars—sometimes more than the down payment!

To help avoid sticker shock, here's what you should be prepared for when closing the purchase of your home.

Estimates of Your Closing Costs

Every good real estate agent should prepare an estimate of your closing costs for you at the time you negotiate your purchase agreement. The really good agents typically can come within 50 bucks of being dead on to the actual costs.

The federal government also requires lenders to prepare an estimate of most of your closing costs, especially loan costs. Called RESPA (Real Estate Settlement Procedures Act), a lender must mail to you a good-faith estimate of what your costs for the loan, and in effect the transaction, will be within three days of your making a formal application for financing. Giving you an estimate, however, does not necessarily mean it will be accurate.

In addition, HUD (Department of Housing and Urban Development) requires that a HUD–1 statement of your closing expenses be given to you, but not until within one day of the final signing or close of escrow. By then, of course, it's usually too late to do anything about the costs. (New requirements for lenders coming out of Congress after the mortgage meltdown of 2007–2008 may also provide additional safeguards for consumers.)

It's important to understand that closing costs are not much regulated. Lenders often charge what they want, leading to so-called garbage fees or unnecessary charges that only benefit the lender. (What garbage fees are is open to interpretation—I give you my take on it throughout this chapter.)

Here's a list of typical closing costs when purchasing a home. (Note: while you probably won't have all of these, you may have most of them.)

Typical Closing Costs Checklist

- Hazard Insurance Policy (fire insurance)
- Home warranty package
- Tax prorations
- Tax service contract
- Mortgage fees
- Attorney fee
- Escrow fee
- Title insurance fee
- A variety of other fees

Most buyers are confused by these fees, so let's go over some of the more common.

> **TIP**
>
> You should have an attorney check over your closing statement before signing it. The attorneys who work in real estate, especially those on the East Coast, usually have set fees for standard transactions. These fees are normally between $1,000 and $1,500 depending on the size and complexity of the deal. Be sure you discuss the fees before hiring an attorney. Remember, the attorney fees, like everything else, are negotiable.

Why Do You Have to Pay for Fire/Hazard Insurance?

As the buyer of a home (new or resale) you will want to (and be required to) carry fire insurance. This ensures that you and the lender, in the event of a catastrophe, will be able to rebuild the home.

Don't think you can save money by just taking a chance and not insuring the property. The lender will demand that you carry minimum fire insurance as a condition of the financing. If you don't, the lender will put its own, usually more expensive, policy on the property and bill you for it. If you refuse to pay, you could be placed in default and the lender could foreclose.

While you are required to pay for fire and basic hazard insurance, you are not usually required to carry a "homeowner's policy" (although some lenders do now require it). The homeowner's policy costs much more than the basic fire/hazard policy, but it's a good investment. It normally protects you against a wide variety of losses, including liability if someone gets hurt on your property.

TRAP

In some areas of the country insurers have been refusing to issue new policies because of losses due to such catastrophes as hurricanes, floods, fires, and earthquakes. Be sure to check to see that you can actually get insurance, or else you may not be able to conclude the purchase of your home! (Many states provide lower cost minimal public insurance when private insurers back out.)

What's a Home Warranty Package?

A home warranty package is optional. It typically costs from $250 upward annually, depending on the quality of coverage.

The plan covers problems from many of your home's systems such as electrical and plumbing that occur after you move in. Most sellers will pay for the first year, to keep you from calling to complain about something such as a leaking water heater. You can usually continue the plan in subsequent years by paying the premium yourself.

Why Do You Have to Pay Taxes on Your Purchase?

It's the only thing that's certain, besides death! You do not have to pay sales tax (at least not yet!) in almost any area of the country, although some states do charge a usually nominal "transfer tax." But you may have to pay property taxes to close the deal.

The escrow company prorates your share of the year's taxes. Proration simply means that if the sellers have already paid taxes in advance, you pay them back for that portion of time that you own the property.

If you are getting a new loan that has a tax impound account, the lender may also require that you pay one or two month's worth of taxes up front to get the account started. (This account pays your taxes for you each year.)

An impound account collects taxes and sometimes insurance costs for you, which **TIP** have been added to your monthly mortgage payment, and then pays these costs annually. If you don't have an impound account, the lender will undoubtedly want you to pay for a tax service contract that will report any time you fail to pay your taxes. This is so the lender can then step in, pay them, and then demand the money from you (on penalty of foreclosure). The fee is usually around $25 to $100. And usually there's no getting out of it!

Why Do You Have to Pay Mortgage Fees?

If you get a new mortgage, you're going to have to pay closing fees on it. These usually comprise the largest part of the closing costs. Often the costs of closing the mortgage can come to as much as 4 or 5 percent or more of the total purchase price. Here are some of the fees and what they represent.

Mortgage Closing Cost Fees Checklist

- **Assumption fee.** If you're assuming an existing mortgage, you will undoubtedly have to pay a fee. It's typically in the $100 or less range. However, most loans today are not assumable.

- **Document preparation fee.** I consider this a garbage fee paid to the lender for preparing the loan documents. Since the lender is making the loan and since it takes only a few taps on a computer keyboard to spit out the documents, in this author's opinion it's absurd to charge a high fee for it.

- **Points.** A point is equal to 1 percent of the mortgage. If the mortgage is for $100,000, 2 points is equal to $2,000. Lenders charge points for a variety of reasons, usually to offset a lower-than-market interest rate that you may be getting. The amount of points you pay varies according to the market. I've seen points as high as 10 or more and as low as zero. Be sure you shop around before you secure financing to find the lender offering the lowest points. The points you pay to get a home loan might be considered interest and may be deductible from your annual income tax. Check with your tax accountant to see how much, if any, of your points may be deductible.

- **Loan fee.** The loan fee is an up-front charge in addition to points. Many lenders, for example, will charge "2 points plus $1,200." The $1,200 is the loan fee and usually goes to cover such work as preparing documents and funding the money. Of course, it's preposterous to pay points as well as a loan fee and a document preparation fee. A good lender will not charge these, or will charge only a minimal loan fee. All the costs should be up front, where you can clearly see them.

- **Account setup fee.** Some lenders may charge you to set up the payback account, the little payment book or monthly invoices you'll get when you pay. This is another garbage fee.

- **Impound account and setup/service fee.** Some loans require you to pay one-twelfth of your taxes and insurance each month. "Impound" simply means the holding of tax and insurance money for you (and then paying it out appropriately). Recent legislation has required lenders to be more scrupulous as to how they handle impound accounts and to demand only a minimum amount of money, usually no more than a month or two, for the account. Some lenders, however, will charge you for setting up this account. Again, to my way of thinking, this is a ridiculous charge.

- **Attorney fee.** If it's your attorney, then of course you will need to pay the fee. On the other hand, if it's the lender's attorney for checking over the mortgage documents and the transaction, it's probably another garbage fee. Unless the deal is unusual in some way, the lender should have attorneys on staff—virtually all do—who automatically check documents and deals. It should be part of the lending service, not a separate charge.

- **Collection setup fee.** A collection setup fee is usually charged if part of the property is a rental and rents need to be collected and paid directly to the lender, or if your payment is going to be paid directly out of your paycheck or checking account to the lender. This fee is atypical and shouldn't appear unless the lender discusses special circumstances with you in advance.

- **Recording fees.** The escrow company charges fees for recording documents. They are usually under $25 apiece. It's a garbage fee if the lender wants to charge you a second time for the same fee.

- **Lender's escrow.** The lender may insist on a separate escrow for the mortgage. If so, this is the fee. Ask in advance and go with a different lender if it is exorbitant.

- **Lender's title insurance.** The lender may require a more comprehensive policy of title insurance called an ALTA. If so, this is the charge.

- **Additional charges** that lenders throw in. Lenders can be very creative in this way.

What Is Title Insurance?

This insures the property against a deficient title from the time you buy it going backward. It means, for example, that if a past seller forged a signature or there was a lien that wasn't paid, the insurance should cover it.

TRAP

There are lots of title insurance companies. Sometimes the real estate agent will prefer a specific company. That may be because the title company is giving perks or because the agent's agency owns the title company. (Perks might be something as innocuous as free stationery.) The relationship between the title company and the agent should be disclosed to you. Since for practical purposes one title company is usually as good as another, it really shouldn't matter to you—except in the case of fees. If one title company is cheaper than another, I would insist on the cheaper company. You must do this at the time escrow is opened. (Many states regulate title insurance fees.)

How Is the Division of Closing Costs between Buyer and Seller Handled?

Usually the party (buyer or seller) who pays for the escrow and title insurance is determined by custom in the particular area. Sometimes it is customary to split these costs down the middle with the seller. Other times, either the seller or the buyer pays most of them. You will be pressured to follow custom for your area. You don't have to, however. Remember, virtually everything is negotiable in real estate.

As part of the escrow charges there may also be other prorations of interest, taxes, rents, and insurance. Just be sure that you're paying only your fair share. Check with your agent, attorney, and accountant if you're not sure.

Items typically are prorated at the close of escrow. However, if you are not getting possession of the property until a later date, then it's usually unfair for you to have to pay interest, insurance, and taxes until that date. If you're taking possession later than the close of escrow, be sure that prorations are made as of that later date.

How Do You Avoid Garbage Fees?

There are two ways, both of which have already been suggested. First, know what the costs and fees should be. If you can't recognize a garbage fee, how can you challenge it?

Second, demand that all garbage fees be eliminated or at the least reduced. However, you must do this at the opening of escrow. If you wait until the last day and escrow is ready to close, trying to make changes could endanger your deal, which could lead to a very angry seller.

If the lender won't dismiss garbage charges when you bring them up at the time of applying for a loan, get a different lender. There are no shortages of lenders in the country.

How Do You Get the Seller to Pay Your Closing Costs?

Remember, everything in real estate is negotiable! That includes closing costs.

To have the seller pay yours, make it a contingency of the purchase. If the seller doesn't pay, you don't buy. The trick, of course, is getting the seller to go along. In a strong market, sellers will simply show your agent (who's presenting the deal) to the door. They won't consider it.

In a weak market, however, where the sellers have been trying unsuccessfully to get out of their house for six months or longer, it often works. The key is to find a seller who's highly motivated to sell. If you're the only buyer to come by in a long while, you may get them to pay your closing costs.

Other considerations are when you're giving that seller a better price than he or she anticipated, or better terms. In a trade-off, the seller might consider paying your closing costs.

TIP

Remember, the closing costs are cash. However, sometimes they can be financed. You offer the seller a good price (assuming the property appraises out) and get a bigger loan. In return, the seller pays your cash closing costs. (Just be sure the lender will go along with this.)

Of course, some buyers who are very tough negotiators argue for it all: good price, good terms, and seller pays closing costs! As I said, in a bad market where houses just aren't selling, sometimes desperate sellers will agree.

How Do You Wrap the Closing Costs into the Mortgage?

Finally, it may be possible to wrap the closing costs into the mortgage. Many lenders in the past and to some extent still today offer "no cost" mortgages. You could opt for one. (Note that we're not talking here about "no down payment" mortgages. We're talking about mortgages with no closing costs.)

A "no cost" mortgage is a misnomer. There are costs. It's just that they are hidden. For example, I recently obtained such a mortgage. At closing, the lender paid all of my NRCCs (nonrecurring closing costs), which included title, escrow, and lender's fees. (It did not, of course, pay my recurring costs such as prorations and hazard insurance.)

In exchange for doing this, the lender increased the interest rate, by ⅜ of a percent.

I had a choice. I could pay the closing costs in cash. Or I could pay a slightly higher interest rate (and slightly higher monthly payment) and have no NRCC.

Another way of handling it is when lenders roll the closing costs into the amount of the mortgage. In other words, they will give you the same interest rate, but you'll end up owing more. The closing costs will be added to the mortgage.

Either way, it's an effective method of reducing the amount of *cash* you have to come up with at closing. Just remember the downside is either a higher interest rate or a bigger loan, both of which usually translate into slightly higher monthly payments.

Closing costs are the bane of real estate transactions. To avoid a bad surprise late in the deal, be sure to get good estimates of what they are early on.

Buy a Lot and Build

Why buy someone else's home, when you can design and build your own?

You'd certainly be the rare person if the thought hadn't at least crossed your mind at some point in your life. It's the secret dream of a great many of us. I know it was the dream of my wife and me when we first did it years ago in the Sierra woods of Northern California. The lessons we learned, as well as those of other self-builders with whom I've talked, can be extremely helpful if you're starting to think more seriously about this.

But Can You Really Do It?

If you think you can, you probably can. It doesn't take as much money as you may think. It doesn't take as much specialized knowledge. What it does take is a lot of time and determination.

TRAP

Chances are you can't do it better than builders whose profession is putting up homes. They know materials and labor, design and construction, as well as where to cut corners and where to be lavish. But what you can offer that they can't is your own unique approach.

I firmly believe that everyone should build their own home, at least once. It's an experience you'll cherish and never forget. And the home you produce will always have a warm spot in your heart.

Start with the Lot

The first thing you must do is find a lot. These days most people who construct their own home do it in rural or vacation areas (developers having already built up most suburban areas). Lots are for sale everywhere, but good lots are hard to find. Here's a checklist of what to look for in a good lot.

Location

Everyone knows that location is important in real estate, but it is doubly important in rural or vacation areas. The reason is simple. Properties here can take much longer to sell (frequently years). If you want to resell, you're going to need a prime location so you can get out relatively quickly. Does your lot have the following (in order of importance)?

	YES	NO
• Water frontage (river or lake)?	[ ]	[ ]
• View?	[ ]	[ ]
• Level building site?	[ ]	[ ]
• Easy access roads?	[ ]	[ ]
• Close to urban/suburban area?	[ ]	[ ]

Lot Amenities

These are the features of the particular lot that you find. Some lots are grand while others are not so grand. Does your lot have:

	YES	NO
• Lots of trees?	[ ]	[ ]
• A lot of room? (Sometimes a minus in the city, but usually a plus in the country.)	[ ]	[ ]
• Good building soil? (It's harder to build in a swamp or "rock country.")	[ ]	[ ]
• A lot of level ground? (It's also harder to build on a mountainside.)	[ ]	[ ]

Watch Out for Poor Soil Quality.   The quality of soil is a critical factor when building. Ideally, you want soil that allows water to percolate yet retains its shape. Expansive soils (mostly clays) expand when they get wet and this can easily lead to cracked foundations. Sandy soils can more easily wash away. Rocky soils often make for good foundations, but are hard to excavate. If there is any doubt at all, get a soils report from a qualified engineering company.

Water

In the city it's something we take for granted, but building in the country, it's a prime consideration. Does your lot have:

	YES	NO
• A well? (Not so good, but better than no water!)	[ ]	[ ]
• A mutual or private water company? (Good)	[ ]	[ ]
• Water for irrigation? (Gardening)	[ ]	[ ]

Watch Out for Wells and Puddles. Beware of lots that have their own wells. Chances are you'll be required to put in a septic tank for sewerage. Unless the lot is very large, the septic leach field may contaminate the well water. In short, it may be difficult to secure a building permit, and even if you do, you stand the chance of poisoning yourself.

Also, many buyers look at their future lot in only one season. In the fall, for example, the lot may be dry and covered with beautiful foliage. However, in the spring, it may be a swamp from stagnant winter rain runoff.

Be sure to talk to local residents to get a picture of what your lot is going to be like all year long. Also look for ditches that neighbors have dug as well as natural water runoffs—these indicate the drainage of the lot. Beware of flat areas with no runoff, as they could become pools of water (or ice) in other seasons.

Sewer System

It's something important to consider before you buy. Does your lot:

	YES	NO
• Have access to a public sewer system? (How much will it cost you to hook up to it?)	[ ]	[ ]
• Require a septic tank? (Do you have enough room for a leach field?)	[ ]	[ ]

Watch Out for Those Leach Fields. "Leach fields" are something new to many first-time home builders in rural areas. If you have a septic system, it is composed of two elements: the tank, which holds the solid sewerage, and the leach field, which drains out the liquid sewerage. A tank takes up only a few dozen square feet. A leach field, on the other hand, requires hundreds of square feet, usually in a flat area. Be sure you have enough room for your leach field as well as your building site when looking at a rural lot. Have the county sanitation engineer check it out.

Power

Yes, many rural or mountain lots have not yet been accessed by the power company. It's a very big negative if it hasn't.

	YES	NO
• Does your lot have electric power?	[ ]	[ ]
• If not, is it coming soon?	[ ]	[ ]

Drainage

This can be a big factor later on, although it's something few of us remember to consider when we buy.

	YES	NO
• Does your lot drain adequately?	[ ]	[ ]
• Are there soft, wet areas indicating heavy water buildup?	[ ]	[ ]
• Will you need to dig drainage ditches before you build?	[ ]	[ ]

Title

Buying a lot is not quite the same as buying a house. You have to worry about all kinds of restrictions.

	YES	NO
• Can you get clear title?	[ ]	[ ]
• Are there any easements (to power companies, water companies, and so on) on your lot?	[ ]	[ ]

- Are those easements just where you want
to build? (If they are, you won't be able to.) [ ]   [ ]
- Are you in any kind of restricted area that
would impair your ability to build, such as:
  ○ A coastal preserve?   [ ]   [ ]
  ○ A national forest?   [ ]   [ ]
  ○ A wildlife preserve?   [ ]   [ ]
  ○ Other?   [ ]   [ ]
- Is there a building moratorium in your area?   [ ]   [ ]

Environmental Concerns

These are important issues that you usually have to dig to discover:

	YES	NO

- Is your area facing any kind of
environmental impact control?   [ ]   [ ]
- Is there something occurring in
the area that would severely affect
the value of your property:
  ○ Draining a lake?   [ ]   [ ]
  ○ Changing the course of a river?   [ ]   [ ]
  ○ Lumbering activity?   [ ]   [ ]
- Is your lot located in a geologically
unstable area (earthquakes)?   [ ]   [ ]

How Are Lots Financed?

Generally lots are paid for either in cash or with a mortgage carried back by the seller (typically for a term of under 10 years at prevailing interest rates). It would be a mistake to buy a lot thinking you can refinance it through a bank. Most lenders won't loan on bare land. Banks, when they will loan, generally will give only 50 percent or less of the appraised value.

Don't be hesitant to make a bold seller financing offer on financing a lot. For example, you may offer 10 percent down with the owners to carry a mortgage for the balance over 10 years at 2 percent below the current interest rate. Remember that lots are hard to sell and that frequently the people who own them, own them free and clear. You're not going to get such a favorable (to you) offer accepted every time, but you will get it accepted more often than you might think.

What About Construction Plans?

Once you have your lot, the next step is to get a set of construction plans. This can be a very expensive or a very inexpensive task. At one end are the ready-made plans which are available through the mail from building magazines (just check your newsstands). At the other end of the spectrum you can hire an architect to draw up a set of plans just for you.

Mail-Order Plans

Mail order is definitely the cheapest way to go, since a set of plans can be obtained for just a few hundred dollars. There are literally thousands of mail-order plans available. Be sure you check to see that they are appropriate for your area of the country and that the building materials list doesn't involve some overly expensive timbers or metal.

Be careful, however, if you buy through-the-mail plans. A "working set" includes all elevations as well as details of all unusual construction. Some of the plans which I have seen sent through the mail are simply a front view and an inside view. They definitely give you enough to see what the house will look like, but they're a far cry from being detailed enough for you or a builder to work with. If you order through the mail, be sure that there is a full "money back" guarantee. In addition, as soon as you get the plans, take them to a builder to see if they are adequate. Expect to pay around $500 for a set of working mail-order plans.

TIP

Even if you order plans through the mail, you will undoubtedly have to modify them to accommodate your building site. You'll need to have them engineered to meet local building codes. And you'll want to alter them to meet your own special needs. Why not hire a local architect on an hourly basis to modify these plans? The cost can be a fraction of what drawing up a set of plans from scratch would be.

Custom-Made Plans

Custom-made is the most expensive way to go, but you can arrive at a unique and well-built house. You hire an architect to draft a set of plans for you. Typically, the cost is 3 to 5 percent of the cost of building the house. (If it costs $200,000 to build the house, figure $6,000 to $10,000 for the plans.)

A good architect will visit the building site and design the plans to fit the contour of the land. In addition, the architect will listen carefully to your desires for a home and incorporate those features that you want.

Finally, a good architect will be aware of building codes and of building materials costs in your area and will design a house to take advantage of whatever cost savings are possible.

Interview the architect as you would any other person you are hiring. Ask to see plans that the architect has previously done. (Sometimes you can save money by modifying an existing set of his or her plans.) Find out who the architect has designed houses for and then call up those owners. Did they like the work? Did the architect take advantage of cost savings wherever possible? Would the owners recommend the person?

Find out first what the costs will be. Some architects work on an hourly basis; others have a set fee. Don't assume that the costs will be minimal. Plans can be very expensive.

Do-It-Yourself Plans

In most areas of the country if you agree to live on the property for at least a year, you are permitted not only to do all or most of the construction yourself but also to draw up the plans. No, this is not an impossible task. I've done it myself and I have no background in architecture or drafting.

What I did was to study the lot and then design a house that took advantage of the view. I then hired a draftsperson to create a set of working construction plans on the basis of my rough sketches.

Finally I hired an engineer to determine the required loads and other engineering features. The total cost to me was under $3,500. You can do it too.

Consult with the Building Department

Work with your local building department, not against it. Find out in advance what special requirements it has (snow load, wind resistance, insulation, sewer systems, and so on). Incorporate these features into your plans at an early stage.

Get to know your local building inspectors and ask for advice. They may save you hours of time and thousands of dollars by suggesting approved methods of building that you may not have thought of yourself.

How Do You Find a Good Builder?

Of course, you can build it all yourself, if you happen to be a relative of Hercules. However, some of the work is extremely hard, such as pouring concrete and lifting heavy timbers. Some requires special skills, such as plumbing, electrical, and plastering. And some is just plain tedious, such as putting up siding and Sheetrock.

The alternative is to hire workpeople and/or a builder. Unless you plan to do at least 75 percent of the work yourself, you're better off striking a deal with a builder. Keep in mind, however, that many builders are interested only in making a set profit on each job. When you submit a set of plans to them for a bid, they simply add up the square footage, multiply by a predetermined price, and that's your cost. You'll be better off with a builder who looks closely at the plans and figures the actual costs unique to your project.

If you plan to do some of the work, finish the house for example, you need to find a builder who actually does true cost estimates. These include finding out what the materials and labor will actually cost and then calculating profit on top of that. In a house I built a few years ago, two builders went the first route, bidding generically just by square footage. The third builder took the other course. The third builder's price was 30 percent lower than that of the first two because he looked closely at actual costs of labor and materials!

Be Your Own Contractor

If you do most of the work yourself, you can hire workpeople to do the remaining chores for you. You can do, essentially, what the builder does. You can hire carpenters, plumbers, roofers, tapers, and so forth.

However, those you hire typically work on a "per job" basis instead of an hourly basis. They will want to see your plans and then will "bid the job." If they see you're inexperienced, they may give you a high bid. To avoid this, be sure that you get at least three bids for each job.

Builder's Qualification Checklist

* How many years has your builder been in the business in the area of your lot? (Three is usually considered a minimum.) _____

	YES	NO
Is your builder state-licensed?	[ ]	[ ]
Have you called the state licensing bureau to see if there are any complaints against your builder?	[ ]	[ ]
Have you called the local better business bureau or district attorney's office to see if there are complaints?	[ ]	[ ]
Have you visited other houses your builder has constructed?	[ ]	[ ]
Did the prior construction look solid?	[ ]	[ ]
Did the owners voice any complaints?	[ ]	[ ]
Did you call the local building supply company to ask if your builder was ever late making payments?	[ ]	[ ]
Is your builder ready and able to get started?	[ ]	[ ]
Do you get along well with your builder?	[ ]	[ ]

TRAP

Most builders will want you to sign a building agreement in which you agree to provide them a series of payments out of which they will pay their workers and their materials suppliers. However, if you pay the builder and the builder does not pay the workers and suppliers, you could still be liable for additional full payment to those workers and suppliers. (They could file mechanic's liens on your property and force payment, forcing you to pay twice!) Your only recourse, in such an event, may be to sue the builder, who may have already filed for bankruptcy. You can help protect yourself, however, by asking your builder to supply you with a completion bond. Most builders balk at this, however, because such bonds tend to be expensive and difficult to qualify for.

If you are securing financing in order to build, generally the lender will check out the builder and will withhold payments until the builder supplies proof of payment for labor and supplies. You can demand this proof (in the form of mechanic's "releases") too.

Again, however, it's a hassle for the builder and many don't like doing it. In addition, sometimes the subs (mechanics) will give releases and then still file liens later on saying that the release was given on the builder's check and the lien was filed when that check bounced!

Probably greater protection comes from insisting on paying subcontractors and materials suppliers yourself. The builder submits a "chit" or authorization and you issue the check.

Again, however, builders don't like doing this because it allows you to see exactly how much they are paying for labor and materials and how much profit they are making on your house. Also, it tends to undermine their authority with the subcontractors.

TRAP

Be sure you understand mechanic's lien laws in your state. Check with a local contractor or, better still, an attorney to get the details.

Be There

You've bought the lot, had the plans drawn up, secured a builder (or hired subcontractors), and are ready to go. Once construction starts, plan on being there a great deal of the time or on having a builder or someone knowledgeable there to handle things.

There are always questions that pop up. What does that little squiggle on the plans mean? The plans call for a 3-foot foundation, but there's a 7-foot hole in the building site—what do we do?

Where do you want the electrical switches? And on and on. Somebody has to be there to handle the questions.

Don't count on the local building inspector to ensure that everything is done right. Building inspectors can't watch everything all the time. If you don't know how it should be built, hire someone who does to supervise the job.

Plan on spending more time than you first estimate. Workers don't show up on time. Building materials are delayed getting to the site. The weather turns against you. To be perfectly safe, use a rule of two. It takes twice as long to do anything than you think it should.

Buying a lot and building your own house is a wonderful experience. But as anyone who has done it will tell you, it's the sort of thing most people only want to do once!

For more information check out my book *Tips and Traps When Building Your Home* (McGraw-Hill, 2001).

Buy a Fixer-Upper

I f you're having trouble finding a home you can afford to buy in the neighborhood you want, then one alternative may be to consider a "fixer." Here you can sometimes substitute "sweat equity" for the cash (or credit/income for loan qualifying) that you need to get in.

A fixer is short for "fixer-upper" (also sometimes called a "handyman special"). It's a house (or condo/co-op) that is in less than perfect condition, sometimes far less. Some merely need paint. Others need a complete makeover. Some even require structural repair. Whatever their deficiencies, they are typically sold at a discount.

Why Should You Consider a Fixer?

Reasons to Buy a Fixer

- Get into an area you'd otherwise not be able to afford
- Get into a house you'd otherwise not be able to afford
- Make a profit

It's Not Simply Cosmetic

My wife and I have a running battle over what constitutes a fixer. She feels that if the paint isn't new and there are one or two cracked counter tiles, it's a fixer. I, on the other hand, maintain that the property has to have a big enough problem that no one will pay full price for it—obsolete kitchen/bath, broken doors in interior, cracked foundation, and so on. Her complaint is that no one will come down on the price for what she considers a fixer. Mine is that they often won't come down far enough to make buying the home and fixing it worthwhile.

Who Should *Not* Consider a Fixer?

It's important to understand at the onset that if you're going to buy a fixer, even if you get it dirt cheap, it's going to cost you time, money, and effort to renovate it. It would be a mistake to buy such a property thinking you can simply move in as you would a house that's already in perfect shape.

If you're the sort that looks at homes and tends to like those which are "ready to go," then chances are you would not be happy with a fixer. In fact, you'd probably walk away from a perfect "fixer" steal simply because you wouldn't recognize it.

Recognizing a Fixer

As suggested above, fixers run the gamut from those that simply need cosmetic work to those that are in such bad shape they need to be "scrapped" (demolished) and a new house erected from scratch.

While most of us would prefer to stay closer to the cosmetic realm, where cleaning, painting, and replacing fixtures are about all we'd be called upon to do, the big discounts come from properties that have more serious problems. For example, at the more serious end of fixers are homes that have broken foundations, have collapsing roofs, have been condemned because of fires or ground shifting, are sliding down hills, and on and on. Homes that have problems this serious will obviously come with a strong discount. Indeed, you may be able to pick up the property for just the cost of the land. In some cases, that's less than half the price for a home in good condition.

Cosmetics versus Renovation in a Fixer

You've got a cosmetic fixer **if**:

- Paint will handle most of the problems.
- New carpeting will do the trick.
- Landscaping the front will be the finishing touch.

You've got a renovation fixer **if**:

- You need to put in a new kitchen and/or bath.
- There are structural problems with the roof, foundation, or framing.
- Major systems (plumbing, heating, electrical) need repair.

Fixing the calamitous problems of a renovator requires ingenuity, money, nerve, and stick-to-itiveness. Unless you have all four, plus a pretty strong background in renovation, my suggestion is that you simply stay away from these. If it's your first time out, you could get burned badly on one of them.

Rather, what you probably want is something closer to the cosmetic fixer. You want a home that looks like a mess, but can be shaped up with lots of paint, simple fixing, and TLC.

Know Your Own Abilities

Perhaps the most important thing when evaluating a fixer is to determine whether you can do the work yourself, or whether it's beyond you. For this reason, it's always a good idea to call in experts—contractors, engineers, agents—people who specialize in fixing the particular problem. In many cases they'll simply give you a bid. In others you may have to pay them a fee. But either way, very often only they can tell you how the problem can be fixed correctly. And how much that will realistically cost.

Where Can You Find a Fixer?

Fixers abound in all communities and in every part of the country. They come about because some people simply never maintain or repair their homes. They let them run down until it's time to sell . . . and they're fixers.

Sometimes it's a case where you have an older home and/or an older owner. The older the home, the more maintenance and repair. The older the owners, the less likely they are able to do this themselves. In some cases the owners die and their property is then disposed of through probate. You can sometimes get a terrific fixer deal in that way.

Other owners, who lose their jobs, get a divorce, or otherwise run into circumstances where they can't keep up the mortgage, lose their property to foreclosure. In a cold market there tend to be far more fixers around because people have let their homes go due to foreclosure.

You can sometimes buy a fixer from a bank or other lender that's an REO (Real Estate Owned). (Check into Chapter 6 for more information on foreclosures.)

And, of course, you can work with agents.

The real trick is separating a hopeless fixer from one that has great potential.

Should You Work with Agents?

Agents are always on the lookout for fixers and if they know that's what you want, most will look for you. However, don't expect agents to fall over at your feet if you tell them you specifically want a fixer. Agents know that good fixers seldom come along and completing a deal on them often takes a lot more work than selling a ready-to-go house.

Check the MLS (Multiple Listing Service), which your Realtor should be able to access. This can take time and careful scouting. However, today the MLS is computerized in almost all areas of the country. You can simply sit down with your agent and use his or her computer's search engine to hunt for suitable properties. (Also check out www.realtor.com, which includes most MLS listings and is available to the public.)

Tips for Finding Fixers on the MLS

Pull the lowest priced listings in each neighborhood. Check for expressions on the listing such as, "needs tender loving care" or "sweat equity opportunity."

Carefully examine the picture. Almost all listings today come with at least one good color image. Does the house look dazzling, as many a fixed up place will? Or does it look a bit tired? Look especially for tall weeds in the front yard, big cracks in the driveway, and temporary cyclone fences. All indicate a problem house.

Check out the "aged" listings. The longer a house has been on the market, the more likely that it has problems. Besides, sellers of homes that have just been listed are unlikely to consider taking price cuts. Usually a seller won't want to reduce the price until a home has sat unsold for a minimum of 60 days or longer.

Ask Your Agent for Help. He or she may well know the area you want to live in. The agent can read the listing, look at the picture, and if the place has been visited, give you a quick synopsis of the home's condition.

Check the "Expireds." If you don't find anything suitable with the current listings, ask to see those listings that have expired. The MLS also carries information on listings that have expired without being sold. This can be a real treasure trove. Listings that have expired are no longer listed for sale. However, often the owners are still willing to sell them. It's just that they've gotten discouraged and have taken the home off the market, often just temporarily. Ask yourself, why did the listing expire? If it was a sharp house, it should have sold, unless the price was unrealistic. Often the reason a home didn't sell is because it's a fixer.

Take Your Time. Be sure you go through *all* the listings. If you're in a metropolitan area that has thousands of listings, it could take days, sometimes a week. But if you find a good fixer, it will be time well spent.

Other Sources of Fixers

Sometimes there are FSBO fixers (FSBO stands for "For Sale By Owner"). A FSBO seller wants to tell you they've got the perfect fixer. But, it's not listed. So, perhaps they've taken an ad in the local newspaper. Perhaps they've put the home on a Web site, maybe even their own. Or perhaps they've written it up on a 4-by-6 card and posted it at a local grocery or drug store.

Where you get the information is irrelevant. I once bought a fixer after meeting the relative of a seller who was sitting next to me on a plane ride! We got to talking, she told me about the house, I made arrangements to see it, the seller and I agreed on price, and within 30 days I owned it!

How Do You Evaluate a Fixer?

Once you've found it, the next question you must answer is, "How much work is required?" That's a lot harder to do than it may at first seem. The reason is that you have to get two important figures. The first is the value of the property *after* it's finished, totally fixed-up.

The second is the amount of money it's going to cost you to do the fixing. Here's the best formula I've found for determining the amount you should offer on a fixer:

Example of Making a Fixer Offer

Value if in perfect shape	$200,000
Less cost of fixing up	−50,000
Less cost to resell	−16,000
Less your time and/or profit	−25,000
Your offer	$109,000

When you think about it, this only makes sense. It's going to cost you money to fix up the property. It will cost money to resell it. And it's only fair that you factor in your time/profit.

TRAP

Don't make the classic mistake of thinking your time isn't valuable. It is. If not spent working on the fixer, you could be earning money elsewhere, or at the very least, relaxing with your family!

Your Costs Will Vary

The cost to fix up depends heavily on how much of the work you do yourself and how much you hire out. My suggestion is that when determining how much to offer, you always base this on hiring everything out. That way, in case you err, you'll at least not be erring on the side of paying too much for the property. If you later do much of, if not all, the work yourself, your savings will be that much more.

How Much Will It Cost to Fix Up?

There is an apparent contradiction in the fact that the house that looks the worst, a cosmetic fixer, often costs the most. The trouble arises from the fact that today sellers are sophisticated enough to know that cosmetic fixes are cheap and easy and they simply don't want to give up any of their profits. Often, in order to get a really good deal, you'll have to buy a house with very serious problems. Of course, that may be simply biting off more than you can chew.

One excellent method here is to line up a series of people in the construction industry who are willing to come out and give you advice. You would, hopefully, have at least the following:

Advisors You May Need

- Carpenter/general contractor
- Plumber
- Electrician
- Roofer
- Carpet layer
- Painter
- Mason (for driveways, paths, foundations)

The problem is getting them to come out and look over a property that you don't yet own. You want them to give you advice, maybe a bid, *before* you buy. In fact, their input will help you to make the purchase decision.

However, their time is scarce and valuable to them and they may be hesitant to come out and give you a bid on a "maybe." That's why it's important to contact these people in advance and try to gain their confidence. Tell them that you plan on using them. If not on this house (because you didn't buy it), then the next one. If they won't budge, and you absolutely need a quick opinion, you might have to pay for their time. Offer them 100 bucks to come out. Yes, it goes against the rules to pay for a bid, but if you need information fast, it can be the right thing to do.

Can You Line Up the Financing?

Financing a fixer can be tricky. Many lenders won't want to give you prime loans on a property that's in bad shape. You'll have to scout out those who will. Your best bet will be banks and the few mortgage brokers (if you can fine one) who specialize in fixers.

Get the Money Up Front

The cardinal rule for financing a fixer is to line up *all* the money you'll need in advance. The reason is that once you get started tearing out walls and flooring, it will be far harder to convince any lender to give you a loan. This means you'll have to calculate pretty closely just how much money it will take to do the entire fix-up.

The Hardest Part

Probably the hardest part of buying a fixer is getting the seller to accept a reasonable price. (Refer to our earlier example for determining how much to pay.) Sellers never want to hear that their property is worth less than they hope to get, even in a down market.

All of which is to say, plan on doing lots of negotiation. And plan on making lots of lowball offers, most of which won't be accepted.

Just be sure that you don't get discouraged and offer more than you should for a property. Once you make your calculations, don't redo them upward because a seller won't budge. Stick with the original figures.

TRAP

It's better to lose a deal, than to get stuck by paying too much.

Don't get discouraged. Lots of people find, buy, and successfully fix up properties every day. There's no good reason you can't be one of them.

Buy a FSBO

f you're house hunting, you owe it to yourself to check out the FSBOs in the area where you want to live. You just might find exactly what you're looking for.

"FSBO" is an acronym for "For Sale By Owner." There are always some FSBOs available in any neighborhood. When the market is hot and houses are selling well, sellers try to avoid paying a commission by selling themselves. When the market is cold and houses aren't selling, sellers eventually give up on agents and try to sell by themselves.

If you decide that you really like a FSBO, then your real work starts—dealing directly with the sellers. Unfortunately, many FSBO sellers have only a vague idea of what the market price for their house should be. Most often they are asking too much. If you suggest this to them, they may be insulted. Thus, sometimes it can be difficult, but not impossible, to negotiate terms or price reductions with FSBO sellers.

Have a Buyer's Agent Help You Out

One way of working the FSBOs is to work with a "buyer's agent." When you find a FSBO that you like, the agent will step in and handle the negotiations. Of course, for his or her role, the agent will expect at least a buyer's agent's commission (usually half of a full commission). Often agents can convince the FSBO sellers to pay this. But if that's not possible, you could be on the hook for it. Be sure you determine in advance how your buyer's agent will handle commissions.

Why Does a Seller Go FSBO?

Almost 85 percent of sellers who start out trying to sell FSBO eventually give up and sell using an agent. Why don't they simply list to begin with and save time?

The answer is that they want to save money. They're hoping that you (or some buyer) will come along and pay them full price, take care of the financing, and let them avoid paying the big 6 percent (or whatever amount) commission to the agent.

What few FSBO sellers recognize is the fact that what's important is selling the home. And trying to get an unrealistic price is wasting their own time. It's wasting your time too.

However, every once in a while, you'll come across a FSBO seller who really wants to sell quickly and understands that by giving you a bargain price, he or she can not only save a little on the commission, but also get a quicker sale. That's the FSBO seller you're trying to find.

You Should Pay Less for a FSBO

Remember, you're not getting the benefit of an agent oiling the waters to make the deal go smoothly. You have to do some of the work or hire an attorney or agent to do it for you. Therefore, there's every reason to expect to pay *less* for a FSBO.

Where Do You Find FSBOs?

Check the Internet first. There are dozens, sometimes hundreds of FSBO sites. Key in the words "FSBO" or "by owner real estate." My personal favorite is www.owners.com. Also check out www.fsbo.com and www.forsalebyowner.com.

In addition, look at www.realtor.com, the official site of the National Association of Realtors. Today, for a few hundred dollars, owner sellers can list their properties using a flat fee MLS listing. Nearly all listings on the MLS also eventually get put on www.realtor.com.

You can also walk the neighborhoods where you want to live and buy a home. Drive the streets. Look for signs that say the house is for sale by owner.

Also check for discount broker signs. Some realties such as "Assist–2-Sell" and "HelpYouSell" will provide signs and some assistance to sellers who are trying to sell by themselves.

Try checking the local newspapers under the head, "For Sale By Owner." Sometimes there will be many ads there, sometimes only a few. If any are in your price range and where you want to buy, call them right up and get out there to look at the property.

Visiting a FSBO

When you do drop by (usually it's best to call first, since many sellers working without agents are wary of strangers), expect to be courteously shown around the property. Unlike when you're touring with an agent, when you can wear whatever you want and act any way you like, when you first meet the FSBO seller, you should be on your best behavior. Dress well. Be polite. Don't hog the conversation. Let the seller give you a tour of the property. Add the complimentary "oohs" and "aahs" at the usual places. In other words, try to make a good impression. Remember, if it turns out that this is the place you want to buy, this seller is the person with whom you're going to negotiate and with whom you're going to take the sales journey.

Take the time to check out the home. Look it over carefully, especially since you won't have an agent along to point out good parts . . . and bad.

If you like the place, I recommend you don't begin negotiations on your first visit. Rather, use that as strictly an exploratory mission. Try to find out as much about the property and the seller's motivation as you can. At the same time the seller will be trying to assess you and your intentions.

Later, after you've left and had a chance to think about it, if you still like the place, call the seller and arrange another time to come down and negotiate. Waiting has the added effect of letting the seller know you're not too anxious. And calling for an appointment allows the seller to build anticipation as to what you might have on your mind, how much you might offer. It gets the seller more interested in seeing what you've got.

Don't Be in a Hurry

Don't plan on simply breezing in, making an offer, and then breezing out. Plan to spend time—hours if necessary. Use "small talk." Get to know the seller better. Let the seller get to know you. When you present your offer, present it one element at a time. Sometimes, if you're lowballing, it's better to present the favorable terms first with the price last. The more time you and the seller spend together, the more likely you are both committed to working out a deal. After all, no one likes to "waste" an entire evening with nothing to show for it. After a while, the seller will begin bending over backward to "save" the deal.

Finding the Enlightened FSBO Seller

Let's say you've dropped in to half a dozen FSBOs and realized that either they weren't for you, or if you liked them, the prices were too high for the market. Now, suddenly, you find a FSBO in the neighborhood and discover the seller is enlightened. He tells you that homes like his in the area go for $300,000. However, he's selling by owner and realizes that's a harder sell. So he'll cut the price by an amount equal to half a commission, $9,000 in a price reduction, if you'll buy directly. The price will be $291,000.

Right off the top you're offered half the value of the commission in a price reduction. Now it's a matter of negotiation. You point out that, yes, you're willing to buy. But since there's no agent, you've got to do all the usual work that the broker performs. Plus, you've got the risks of dealing directly with a seller. You want a price reduction equal to at least the full commission.

The seller balks, and maybe you compromise somewhere in between. Or, maybe he agrees. Remember, he's keeping his eye on the donut and not the hole. He wants the sale.

If all goes well, you'll get the home at a lesser price.

How Do You Handle Paperwork in a FSBO Deal?

The correct answer is, "Very carefully!"

You can't trust an inexperienced seller and one who probably lacks the knowledge to handle the paperwork for the transaction. This is an area that tolerates few mistakes. The wrong language, a misinterpretation of a law, the failure to include some important item such as your demand for a professional home inspection, could result in a bad deal that could hurt you or might end up in litigation. You want it done right.

In actuality an enlightened FSBO seller will already have considered this problem and come up with a viable solution. That solution, usually, is to have an agent prepare the purchase agreement and other paperwork on a fee-for-service basis. Alternatively, the seller may be having an attorney do it.

On the East Coast, the usual price for having a real estate attorney handle all the paperwork in a typical transaction is between $750 and $1,500 (depending on what's involved). Today the many new fee-for-service agents charge similar amounts. Keep in mind, however, that while attorneys who handle real estate transactions are found all over the East Coast, they are seldom found in other parts of the country. Fee-for-service agents, however, are cropping up everywhere.

If the seller hasn't come up with this solution, you can come up with it yourself. Just be sure that you agree in advance who will pay the costs of having the paperwork done.

What About Arranging for Inspections and Getting Repairs Done?

That's what the agent does. No agent? Then it's up to you or the seller. It's a good idea to get an initial understanding between yourself and the seller on the delegation of responsibilities. The last thing you want is to think the seller is doing something important while, in reality, she thinks you're handling it.

Your fee-for-service agent, your attorney, or your escrow officer can come up with a good list of things that need to be done in order to close your particular escrow. Then, delegate who will do what.

But be sure to call the seller occasionally to see that she is doing her part. You don't want to come to the end of escrow only to discover that the seller hasn't even started with termite repair work.

Can You Negotiate with a FSBO Seller?

Yes, but usually with some difficulty. Face-to-face negotiations are something that most of us cringe at. Yet, to get a home at a better price by buying a FSBO, it's something we'll have to do. Here are some helpful points to remember:

FSBO Negotiating Tactics

- **Remember this is business.** Never say anything personally disparaging to the seller. To do so will almost immediately end the negotiations. If the seller says something personal against you, make note of it, and then move on. If you hold it personally against the seller, again, the deal's likely to come unraveled.

- **Argue at your peril.** Always remember that if you argue with the seller, there's no third party to settle the argument. You could each end up in a rigid, uncompromising position that would make consummating a deal impossible. Instead simply listen to the seller and then present your position. If you're at odds, then look for common ground and whittle away the disagreement until you're both in agreement. Sound easier than it is? Perhaps, but with a little practice and keeping a cool head, it works surprisingly well.

- **Never lie, not even a tiny, little small one.** If you have a credit problem, you don't necessarily have to bring it up. (Although if it's going to affect the deal, getting it out in the open early usually is a good idea.) However, once it comes up, don't lie about it. Don't make it bigger than it is, but don't make it smaller either. Lies, even small ones, have a way of poisoning the negotiation. If the seller catches you in a lie, he or she begins wondering what else you're lying about. Maybe you're just there to cheat the seller? Maybe you really don't have the cash to buy or can't qualify for the mortgage? And on and on. Telling the truth may hurt, but it hurts a lot less than lying.

- **Don't argue price.** When the seller's price is way off, let him know. But back your comments up with facts. Have a list of recent comparable sales in the area to point to. Let the facts do the work for you. Figures don't lie. They tell what the house is worth.

Get It in Writing

You may be agreed on Monday morning. But by Thursday morning the seller may be having second thoughts and want to start negotiations all over again.

Get yourself immediately down to an attorney or agent who'll write up the deal, and then get everyone's signature on it. Only then can you breathe a conditional sigh of relief (conditioned on the deal finally closing some 30 days later after you get financing, the seller clears title, and everything else goes according to plan).

Buy a New Home

A question frequently asked by buyers is, "Where will I get the greatest appreciation—in a new home or in a resale?" (Or in a bad market, which home holds up its value the best?) To put it another way: "If I had a choice between two houses, a brand new one and a resale, each worth $200,000 and both in similar neighborhoods, which house would make me the most money or cost me the least money over the next five years?"

In the distant past the answer was generally the resale. The existing house had developed neighborhoods, schools, shopping, parks, and so on. It had all the amenities already in place, and for that reason resales tended to appreciate more than new homes . . . and to cost more as well.

Recently, however, the tables have turned. During the last downturn in the market, builders were so intent on getting rid of inventory that they cut prices to the point where they were offering outstanding bargains, often eclipsing what could be found in the resale market. Thus buying new, if you can get a bargain, often makes great sense.

Of course, many people buy new homes more than just for their potential price appreciation. Here are some typical reasons:

New or Resale?

Buy a new home

- If you don't want to inherit maintenance and repair problems.
- If you want to move into a "clean" house where everything is spotless and new.
- If you don't mind putting in backyards, fences, lawns, and otherwise completing the development of the property.

Buy a resale

- If you want to live in a "proven" neighborhood (established schools, crime rates, and so on).
- If you desire a mature area (lots of trees and shrubs).
- If you want "character"—Victorian, New England, Spanish, Plantation, or other style.

Important Considerations

Consider Neighborhood First

A resale has a proven neighborhood—you know what it looks like. A new home only has a hoped-for neighborhood. Maybe it will turn out great . . . and maybe not.

If it were me, I would shop neighborhood first.

Consider Lot Size

Land is the single most expensive part of a home. Therefore, to conserve on land, today's builders often put large homes on postage-stamp-sized lots. If you like a lot of privacy and space, consider a resale. The older home usually will offer you more land.

Consider Home Size

On the other hand, newer homes tend to be far larger than their earlier cousins. Today's buyer wants a larger home. And the feeling seems to be, "Who cares about a small lot, as long as I have a big house!"

Real estate is a localized market. That means that you cannot say that something is true at any given time for *all* parts of the country. While Southern California, for example, or New York may see property values level off, at the same time parts of the Midwest or South may see them plummet . . . or vice versa.

How Do You Find the Right New Home?

If you're determined to buy a new home, be prepared to spend some time looking. In most areas of the country, the era of the huge tract has given way to smaller, condensed tracts built a phase at a time.

To see all of the new homes in your area, you may have to spend time traveling. Many areas have a "buyer's guide" to new homes—a small magazine detailing the houses and their price ranges and showing maps of how to get there. The Sunday real estate section of any major newspaper almost always has ads for new homes.

What Should You Look For in a New Home?

Here's a checklist of items to look for when choosing a brand-new home:

New-Home Checklist

- **Number of bedrooms.** Three or four is often best for resale; two may restrict your ability to resell quickly; five could make the house overbuilt for the area. _____
- **Number of bathrooms.** Two is minimal, three is better, four could be overkill. _____
- **Ceilings.** High ceilings are in vogue. A better house will have at least one room with vaulted ceilings, usually a living or family room. _____
- **Kitchen.** Large and well-equipped kitchens sell houses. If your kitchen has an island in it complete with a stove, all the better. Is the oven self-cleaning? _____
- **Garage.** A two-car garage is a must. Three-car is better. _____
- **Additional rooms.** These are a plus, if they don't force the price out of sight. They include library, nursery, computer room, even a home theater. _____
- **Yard.** Small yards are the rule today, given the high cost of land. Many families actually prefer small yards to avoid having to do extensive yard work. People with children, however, usually like larger yards. Large yards are considered luxury items and are found in more expensive homes. _____
- **Central air-conditioning.** More and more it is considered to be a necessity, rather than a luxury. _____
- **High-quality insulation.** Check with the builder. The "R" rating should be the minimum required for the weather in your area. Higher "R" ratings will decrease your heating

and cooling costs. Ask if the house was "wrapped" with a vapor/moisture barrier. It helps the insulation do its work. _____

- **Glass.** Are the sliding glass doors, bathroom windows, and other windows that are easily accessed by children made of "safety glass"? _____
  ◦ Are they double-pane? _____
  ◦ Low-E? (indicating a high insulation value) _____
- **Electrical outlets.** The standard in most construction is one outlet every 12 feet of linear wall space. Extra outlets in kitchens and baths are a plus. GFI (ground fault interrupter) plugs in wet areas such as kitchen or bath are a safety must. _____
- **Floor coverings.** Wall-to-wall carpet is the rule in most new homes. Tiles are a plus. Hardwood floors are an additional plus, but remember, you'll probably want to buy carpet to put over them. _____

How Do You Check Out a Neighborhood?

It's hard with a new home because frequently the neighborhood is likewise new and undeveloped. Here's a checklist to help you evaluate a neighborhood for a new home.

New-Home Neighborhood Checklist

	YES	NO
• Are the local schools good? (You can ask to see their scores on standardized tests to judge.)	[ ]	[ ]
• Are the schools nearby?	[ ]	[ ]
• Are there day-care facilities nearby?	[ ]	[ ]
• Is the area relatively crime free? (Check with the police department's Public Affairs officer, who can usually give you crime statistics down to the block.)	[ ]	[ ]

	YES	NO
• Does the police department seem responsive?	[ ]	[ ]
• Is there adequate fire protection? (Check with your insurance company for fire ratings in the area.)	[ ]	[ ]
• Is shopping nearby?	[ ]	[ ]
• Is there a hospital nearby?	[ ]	[ ]
• Is the neighborhood "quiet"? (Come back at different times of the day to check.)	[ ]	[ ]
• Are nearby posted speed limits slow? (You want a 25 mph limit, not 35 or 45.)	[ ]	[ ]
• Is there a high-traffic street nearby that cars shoot out of?	[ ]	[ ]
• Is there a park nearby?	[ ]	[ ]
• Is public transportation available?	[ ]	[ ]
• Is there adequate off-street parking?	[ ]	[ ]
• Are the lots "private" enough?	[ ]	[ ]
• Is the tract landscaped? Will it be by the builder?	[ ]	[ ]
• Is there danger of future erosion? (If you're not sure, check with a soils engineer.)	[ ]	[ ]
• Does the water system provide pure drinking water? (The water company almost always must supply you with the results of water purity testing.)	[ ]	[ ]
• Are there any special assessments that you'll have to pay (street improvement, sewer tax, and so on)?	[ ]	[ ]
• Are there any nearby hazards or nuisances (factories, swamps or rivers, oil tanks, hazardous waste facilities, and so on)?	[ ]	[ ]
• Are the homes connected to a sewer system (septic systems are less desirable)?	[ ]	[ ]

In addition to the features of the house itself as well as the neighborhood, there is the factor of the new-home market. The housing market is volatile, with many ups and downs. Here's what to look for.

How Do You Judge the New-Home Market?

In a slow market, typically there are more new homes than buyers, and builders are anxious to sell them off. The ads for the homes are placed in all papers, there are signs along the major roads directing you to the new tracts, and there are almost always models of all the homes available to see. And in a down market, there are lots of foreclosures available.

TIP

As a rule, new homes will have newer and more efficient heating and cooling systems, more insulation, better windows (double pane and low-E), tighter weather stripping, and so on. This all translates into lower energy costs, a plus for you.

While the salespeople in the office try to get you to make a quick decision, remember that you usually have plenty of time. You can leisurely shop around, going from model to model until you find just the right home for you. Once you find it, you can often negotiate more favorable terms from the builder (reduced price, a buy-down on the loan—where the builder pays part of your interest for a few years—free amenities such as fences, yards, and so forth).

This is the ideal market in which to buy a new home. You're sitting in the driver's seat.

Try to find a small to medium-sized home in the best-located tract—this property will often appreciate the fastest. (Beware the very smallest home as it simply may be too small for many buyers when it comes time for you to sell; the largest home is often too expensive when it comes time for resale.)

What If We're in a Real Estate Recession?

You'll know a depressed market if you're in it. Every Sunday the paper will offer "repos" and "REOs" and "bank-owned properties" for sale or auction. If the ads don't alert you, there are other signs of a down market such as statistics available from brokers and published in the business section of the local papers. These indicate that the volume of home sales is dramatically down from the previous year. Or the number of houses advertised for sale (both new and resale) in the newspapers is enormous. Or most importantly, tracts of new homes are fully built with the houses standing vacant and unsold.

Don't buy on the way down. Be wary of buying a new home in a real estate recession. In a down market you can find apparent "steals" as desperate builders fight to get out. However, how wise is it to buy today, when you might buy the same house for less tomorrow?

Remember, often it's not how much you pay, it's when you buy and sell. Markets go both ways. Sometimes the most important thing is knowing when to move quickly and when to wait before you buy.

Should You Buy a Not-Yet-Built Home?

You may have a choice between buying an already built home or one that a builder has yet to put up. There are pros and cons with going either way.

With the already built home, you know what you're getting and usually can see the neighborhood. But with the not-yet-built home, items can be changed to fit your specific needs.

My suggestion is that whenever possible always buy a home that is already built. I believe that knowing what you're going to get is more important than being able to customize a plan. Besides, you know for certain that it's actually going to get built.

What If the Builder Is Slow or Stops Construction?

You can't make a builder go faster, or put up a home when he or she stops work. Usually, tardiness or a halt in construction is caused by circumstances beyond the builder's control, such as problems with financing, labor troubles, or problems with the local building department.

THE "COMING SOON" SYNDROME

A friend of mine wanted to buy a new home in a development in Orange County, south of Los Angeles. Jill loved the location and fell in love with one of the models. There were several homes already constructed and ready for sale, but not the model she wanted. The builder told Jill that her model would be available in the "next phase." He took a $500 refundable deposit from her and signed an agreement, explaining that she would be required to fill out a sales agreement as soon as the house was built. The $500 merely reserved the house for her. He guessed that it would be ready in 4 months.

Four months later the builder hadn't even broken ground. Jill and a number of others were haunting his offices trying to find out what the problem was. All she could get were vague answers.

She was told that the lenders would not agree to the financing because of some title problems. Or there was a permit difficulty with the city. Or the builder was waiting until materials costs came down. Or something else.

Finally, 5 months after Jill paid her deposit, work began. It took another 8 months to finish her home.

During the building period, she visited the home whenever she could, sometimes several visits a week. She didn't notice any problems until the house was almost completed and the wallboards were put up. Then she realized that the floor plan was not exactly the same as the model. The windows of the living room didn't face the hills, the one feature she admired most about the plan.

She confronted the builder. Yes, he explained, the plans were changed. Building costs had changed and he was just adjusting to them. A few corners had been cut here and there so that he could deliver the property at the agreed-upon price. What could she do? She continued to wait.

Finally, the building was completed. It wasn't at all what Jill hoped it would be. But after all the waiting (nearly 11 months), she was glad she would be able to move in.

When she went to sign the sales agreement, however, she found that the price had gone up by $15,000! "How could that be?" she wanted to know. She had agreed upon a price with the builder. He pointed out that the price he agreed upon was the price of 11 months earlier. Costs had gone up since then, both building materials and labor. She didn't expect him to sell for yesterday's price, did she? He pointed to a clause in their agreement that clearly stated he could adjust the price.

In the end, it wasn't the house Jill wanted at the price she wanted to pay. She got her $500 deposit back and began to look elsewhere. However, she had lost nearly a year, not to mention all the hassle.

No, it doesn't happen all the time. It probably doesn't happen most of the time (although price and plan changes are legend in construction). But it does happen enough that you should be aware of it and at least plan on the possibility.

Don't Forget the Upgrades

You'll quickly discover that when you buy a new home there are plenty of upgrades available. Here's a list of some of the upgrades you can typically expect to pay more for:

Common Upgrades

- Larger lot or lot with a view
- Any changes in the basic construction plan
- Landscaped yard
- Better roof
- Better carpeting or tile
- Air-conditioning (now standard on many homes)
- Additional mirrors or windows
- Better appliances (stove, oven, dishwasher, refrigerator)
- Better fixtures (toilets, sinks, tubs)
- Larger water heater

What's interesting is that while you may have your choice of a variety of upgrades, chances are you'll only be able to choose from the builder's list at the builder's price. For example, you may have your choice of three grades of carpet and that's it. Or you can choose from six tile patterns, three of which cost extra, no other changes may be allowed.

You don't like what the builder offers? And chances are you don't like the upgrade prices. So what do you do? The most logical thing is to tell the builder no thanks and that you'd like an allowance for his cost of materials. You'll go out and buy your own. Not a chance (in most cases)! Most builders will *not* give you an allowance against standard items.

There are several reasons that builders limit the changes and upgrades you can make. One is cost. They get guaranteed estimates from a few distributors and they know what it's going to cost to purchase a particular product. That makes it easy for them to stick with that product.

Also, there's the cost of labor as well as materials. Some materials require extra labor costs. For example, some Mexican tiles are irregular (when compared with American or European tiles), and there may be an extra labor charge for installing them. To avoid hassles here, the builder may simply limit the selection to half a dozen patterns, all because he knows he can control the labor costs.

Finally, there's the matter of lender and building department approval. The builder usually has lenders who have guaranteed approval of financing, provided the house is built a certain way with certain features. Change the features and a new appraisal might be necessary. Similarly, the plans may call for specific features. Change those features and the builder may have to submit new plans to the building department.

TRAP

Did you know that many building departments will not give final approval to a home until all the carpeting, appliances, and fixtures are in? Thus, even if you want to buy upgrades on your own, the builder can't agree to it and still "final" (get a notice of completion and occupancy signed off from the building department) the home.

The real question you should ask yourself is: Which upgrades and extras are worthwhile and which are not? Here are some clues.

Is a Larger or View Lot Worth It?

If the price isn't that much more, go for it. For example, a lot with a view or a larger lot may cost 3 to 15 percent more than a standard lot. Usually this will pay in the long run. On the other hand, back off if the price is excessive. Keep in mind that if you buy a view lot, it may be the best money you can spend. If you're in an area where view lots are prized, you could get it back many times over when you sell.

On the other hand, beware if you buy a larger lot. Unless you landscape it so that it requires little to no maintenance work, it could be a drawback when you resell.

Is It Worthwhile to Upgrade Carpets and Floor Coverings?

Usually new homes come with wall-to-wall carpet, tile, and/or finished wood. But the quality of these often leaves much to be desired. The difference is most obvious with carpets and tiles. The model home may have luxurious, thick carpeting, whereas the actual carpeting that comes with your home may be short and skimpy. The model may have colorful Italian tiles while the standard home comes with ordinary white tiles.

I've found that it usually doesn't pay to upgrade floor coverings *if* the builder is charging a hefty price for the privilege. In too many cases you can go out and buy the same upgraded floor covering for a fraction of the builder's price. Better to just live with the standard grade and then, after a year or two, replace it.

On the other hand, if money is no object and you want better floors, go for it.

Should You Pay for an Upgraded Yard?

Many homes these days come with a landscaped front yard. Almost none come with landscaped side and backyards. However, your builder will usually put these in for you, for a price.

This is usually an expensive trap. Putting in yards can be very costly. On the other hand, if you do some of the work yourself and hire out only the difficult tasks like installing the watering system and planting large trees, you can do it for significantly less.

Should You Upgrade to Air-Conditioning?

Most new houses in the southern part of the country offer this as standard. If air-conditioning is offered as an upgrade (instead of a standard feature), I would get it. The climate appears to be growing warmer in most parts of the country. Today, just as in automobiles, air-conditioning is considered to be a necessary feature. You may find that you have trouble selling your house later on if it doesn't have air.

What About Other Upgrades?

It all depends on what they cost, how much better they make the house look, and how much more livability they add. My own rule-of-thumb is to go for upgrades whenever they are inexpensive and leave them off whenever the price is exorbitant.

How Can You Watch Out for Shoddy Construction?

One of the advantages of buying a resale is that you pretty well know what you're getting. If the home has been standing for 5, 10, or more years, chances are it will stand another 30 or 40.

On the other hand, when you purchase a new home, you're buying something that is as yet untried. If there are defects, they could show up in the first few years of usage.

"But," I hear many readers saying, "Aren't new homes fully inspected by city or county building departments? Don't they have to meet strict health and safety guidelines?"

Yes . . . and no. All modern buildings are inspected at numerous times during their construction. In most cases, the inspector catches problems and forces their correction before a "certificate of occupancy" is granted. (You can't occupy the home without this certificate—in most areas you can't even connect to water, power, or gas without it.)

However, there may be only one or two building inspectors and hundreds of houses to inspect. Further, while in most cases the inspectors are well trained and experienced, they often are not expert in every area of construction. And in a few cases they simply are not very well qualified.

The upshot of all this is the fact that, regardless of the area of the country, shoddy construction goes on all the time right next to excellent construction. For example, a few years ago the builder of a housing tract in Southern California decided to use a Spanish tile roof. This consists of red, curved tiles interlaced to form a very attractive roof line.

The trouble with the tiles is that they aren't very good at holding out water. In a wind-driven storm, the water sweeps up under the edges of the tiles and through the roofs. In the old days (the 1700s) Spanish tile roofs were used extensively in California. However, in those days a kind of mortar was applied to the roof and the tiles were carefully set into it. This effectively waterproofed them.

Today the use of this mortar would be unattractive and expensive. So instead, roofers lay down layers of heavy, waterproof felt before placing the tiles. It acts as an effective water barrier.

However, in this particular tract the roofer had never before laid Spanish tiles. No felt was placed beneath them. The building inspector, also unfamiliar with the need for felt, didn't catch it.

You're right. With the first rain the roofs leaked—every roof in a tract of over 60 houses! About two-thirds had been sold and the water damage forced the occupants out. Needless to say, they were furious and everyone looked to the builder for repairs. The builder was an honorable person, but not particularly wealthy. All the tiles on the roofs had to be removed and felt placed underneath. It meant reroofing over 60 homes—a very, very costly thing to do. The builder simply couldn't handle it and declared bankruptcy.

Note, this was shoddy construction. But no one was really trying to cut corners. It was just a case of a builder working in an area of unfamiliarity and a building inspector likewise being in the dark.

Of course, this is a dramatic exception. Most buyers of new homes have no problems at all (or small problems which the builder quickly fixes). But that doesn't mean that major structural problems in workmanship or even materials couldn't occur. In a way it's like buying a car. Chances are the one you get will be wonderful. On the other hand, you could get a lemon.

What About Builder Warranties?

Most builders back their construction with warranties. Even a builder who does not give you a written warranty may be offering you an "implied" warranty, depending upon the state in which you live. Today many states have strong consumer protection laws that allow you to take the builder to court for shoddy construction and win a settlement. (Of course, that's of dubious value if the builder has gone broke.) Often the warranties run for 10 years or more, although specific types of repairs or replacements may be limited to only one year.

Of that vast majority of builders who offer warranties, there are two groups: those who self-warrant and those who buy insurance.

Self-Warranted Homes

A builder who self-warrants a home will normally give you a certificate of warranty, which states what is covered and what is not covered. Typically such a warranty says that if it's not specifically noted, it's not covered.

The Magnuson-Moss Act (1975) is a disclosure law that is handled by the Federal Trade Commission (FTC). Under Magnuson-Moss, a warranty may entitle you to specific protections. They should include the following:

What to Look For in a Builder's Warranty

- The name of the person who is warranted (you) and a specific statement of whether the warranty is transferable if you sell the property.
- Precise information on what is covered and what is excluded.
- Exact language detailing what a builder will do to correct a problem that arises.
- The length of the warranty.
- The procedure, in detail, for filing a claim.
- Any limitations on consequential damages. (Consequential damages result as a consequence of covered problems. The most common example is a water pipe bursting and causing damage to furniture. The pipe may be covered, but is the furniture?)
- A clear statement of any reduction of implied warranties.

TRAP

As part of the warranty, some builders have the buyers sign a statement that they waive all implied warranties. In the states that permit this, if you sign such a statement, you may give up more rights than you get, since the implied warranties may be stronger than the builder's specific warranties. If a builder insists you sign a waiver statement, you may want to consider a different builder and house. At least check it over with your attorney.

Under a builder's warranty, you have to go back to the builder to get satisfaction if a problem arises. It's to your advantage, therefore, to find a builder that is big enough to sustain the losses involved with any likely problems.

Insurance-Warranted Homes

A different kind of warranty is offered by a large group of builders nationwide. This is a warranty backed not only by the builder but also by an insurance company. Typically under these policies the builder continues to warrant the house, but the insurance company backs up that warranty. In addition, it often offers a plan that changes with the years the house is in existence, offering greater protection in the first years and less in the later ones.

Many insurance-backed warranties are transferable. However, there may be limitations and exclusions. Usually under these plans, your first recourse is to seek a solution to the problem from the builder. If the builder does not or is not able to comply, the insurance company picks up the tab for covered items after a deductible is paid.

Should You Get a Home Inspection?

Yes. Just because it's a new home, doesn't mean that it's built right. You should have it inspected both before you move in, and, if possible, several times during the construction phase. A good builder will not only allow you to do this, but will encourage you to do it.

A professional home inspector should be able to give you all sorts of help here. You'll want someone with a strong construction background who can check everything from the pouring of the foundation to electrical, plumbing, roofing, drywall, and finishing.

Don't make the mistake of confusing "new" with "good." Yes, it may be good work . . . but then again, it just might not be.

How Do You Find a Good Builder?

Most of us simply shop houses. We go from tract to tract trying to find the new home that will be just right for us. It's also important, however, to shop builders. As should be evident from the discussions on shoddy workmanship and on warranties, a lot depends on the builder. You want a builder who does good work and who has the means to back it up should any unforeseen problems arise.

Here's a checklist to help determine the quality of the builder.

Checklist for Selecting a Good Builder

- How long has the builder been constructing new homes? (Longevity is always a good sign.)
- Can you get a recommendation (or a condemnation!) from a relative, friend, or associate who's previously had dealings with the builder?
- Check with the Better Business Bureau. This organization normally keeps complaints filed against businesses. Does the builder have many complaints filed?
- Check with any consumer groups active in the area. Also check with the local office of the National Association of Home Builders. Your builder may be a member of this group and it may be able to give a recommendation.
- Find out where the builder has previously built new homes. Go to the tract and knock on a few doors. Simply say you are going to be buying a home from the same builder and you would like to know if those who bought before had any difficulties, such as shoddy work or reluctance to fix problems. Don't be embarrassed. Homeowners love to talk about their builder. Either she's wonderful and has done a marvelous job. Or he's been a disaster for them. Just be sure you talk to more than one person to get a balanced viewpoint.

Can You Negotiate Price with the Builder?

Now we come to the tricky part for many new-home buyers: negotiating with the builder. Here many who purchase a new home are completely lost, signing anything and everything that is placed before them.

Just as with purchasing a resale, when buying a new home everything is negotiable. The problem with new homes, however, is that the builder is often tied into financing and labor and materials contracts so that he or she cannot really offer the flexibility that an owner of a resale can.

Typically, when buying a new home, you are presented with a colorful and expensive-looking brochure which gives the floor plans of the various models that the builder is offering. Along with these is usually a price schedule. For Plan A the price is $185,000 until January 2, when the price goes up to $187,500. For Plan B the price is $235,000. For Plan C it's $268,000. And so forth.

In addition, there are premiums for better lots as well as additional costs for upgrades, as described earlier. Thus, the prices are laid out in the same fashion as they are in a grocery store. You certainly can't bargain with the grocer over the price of a jar of mayonnaise. How do you bargain with a builder over the price list for a new home?

Don't Get Suckered

It's important to understand that builders and developers like to create the impression that nothing is negotiable—either you take their price or you don't get the house. That's part of the reason for the elaborate brochures. The truth, however, is that builders are real estate sellers just like any other. When builders need to get rid of homes, they will negotiate down to the bare bones, regardless of what the brochures say.

The way you negotiate with builders is to say that you would "like to submit an offer on one of the houses." The tract salesperson should be a licensed real estate agent and he or she, acting as a fiduciary for the builder, must submit all offers (unless the builder has stipulated that no offers be submitted below a specific price—an unlikely possibility). A better way is to have a buyer's agent do the negotiating for you. However, here you could be liable for a commission.

The easiest way to negotiate is to find a builder who already has houses up and may even be facing foreclosure on some of them. This builder is paying a hefty finance charge each month the houses remain unsold. This builder is highly motivated to sell the property.

However, as noted, builders may not have a lot of wiggle room with regard to price, even when the market's down. They usually have enormous flexibility, however, when it comes to upgrades.

Yes, you say you'll pay their price, or close to it. But you want an upgrade of carpet at no additional cost to you, and you want a self-cleaning oven instead of the standard oven included with the home, and you want floor to ceiling mirrors in the bathrooms and on and on.

Remember, the builder gets the upgrades wholesale. If he or she simply passes them on to you at cost, it probably won't be a hardship to the builder. And it could save you thousands.

On the other hand, don't expect the builder to budge when the houses haven't yet been constructed. In this case, there's no leverage on your side. Why should the builder accept a lower offer when she hasn't even put up the houses and isn't paying interest on them?

Don't Forget to Bargain on Terms

This is often the case when interest rates are higher and it's difficult for buyers to qualify for mortgages.

The builder may be willing to "pay down" the mortgage by several points. For example, you'll get the mortgage. However, instead of paying the going rate of, say, 7 percent for the first 3 years, you might pay 4 percent, with the builder paying the other 3 percent. It can be a great savings to you.

TRAP

Beware of builders who pay down the mortgage just to raise the price by an offsetting amount.

In most cases, a builder won't buy down an interest rate unless the houses have been sitting around for a while and high interest rates are keeping buyers away.

TIP

By talking to those who bought six months ago in the same tract, you should be able to establish what the original pricing was. Thus, you can determine if the builder has raised the price to pay for your buydown.

Buy a Condo or a Co-op

For many people, there is no choice to make, they simply want a single-family house. That's all they've had in the past and nothing else will do.

Others insist on a condo or co-op. Typically they look forward to the maintenance-free lifestyle it offers.

Most people, however, are at least somewhat open to either. Usually the big concern is financial. If homes are expensive, will a condo/co-op be cheaper to buy? Will prices appreciate (or drop) faster in a condo/co-op than a single-family house? Are there any real differences?

Price Appreciation in Condos versus Single-Family Homes

Going back about 50 years the rule-of-thumb was that when prices went up, condos were the last to appreciate. When prices fell, they were the first to go down. That changed during the real estate bubble when, in many parts of the country, condominium price appreciation actually exceeded that for single-family homes! Indeed, in many areas condos sold quicker and for more money per square foot than their single-family counterparts.

TRAP

Always compare apples with apples. When comparing prices between condos and single-family homes, do it on a square foot basis. If a 2,000-square-foot house is selling for $300,000 and a 1,500-square-foot condo is selling for $250,000, which costs more for what you get? The answer is the condo! The condo is selling for $167 a square foot, the home for $150 a square foot. It's something to consider.

The reason condos appreciated faster than in the past is mainly because there were fewer of them available. Thirty years ago, builders swarmed to condominium construction and conversion. (A conversion is where an apartment building is converted to condominiums.) For the builders, the costs were less than for single-family homes, yet the prices they could get were handsome. So they built condos.

Then came the lawsuits. As it turned out, builders had grabbed hold of the tail of a tiger. When the roof on one or two units leaked, the HOA (Homeowners Association) often demanded the entire roof over all the units be replaced, before leaks could appear elsewhere. When the ground settled under the building, the HOA sometimes demanded the whole building(s) be lifted and a new foundation poured. Similarly, problems were found with plumbing, electrical, mold—all matter of things. Since the builders often had to guarantee the construction for at least 10 years (in some cases by state law), they were faced with enormous liability.

Some builders went out of business. Others took the heavy financial hit. But very few built more condos. In California, as an example, in 1999 there were roughly 20,000 new condo units built. By 2002 that number had dropped to roughly 2,000.

As a result, in many areas there was a shortage of condominiums. And, consequently, the price of those available was driven higher.

TRAP

When buying a condo, it's often best to look for units that are at least 10 years old and that don't have any pending lawsuits. Chances are any construction problems will have already been taken care of. And you won't risk buying into assessments if the existing lawsuits go against the homeowners.

Today's Market

When the real estate market turned down in 2007, the condo market was no exception. Sales plummeted and, shortly afterward, so did prices.

Did condos do better than single-family detached homes? In some areas yes, in others no. Today, condos are about on a par with individual homes in most areas. A condo remains about as good an investment as a house, but probably no better.

What Is a Condo?

A condominium, as most buyers know, involves shared ownership. You end up with a deed to the property (called a "fee simple") and separately own the inside of the unit while sharing with the other owners the grounds, walkways, and recreational facilities—in short, everything outside.

Another way to look at it is as if you were renting an apartment and then decided to buy your rental unit. (Indeed, some condos are converted apartment houses.)

It's sometimes useful to know that there are actually two separate kinds of condominium ownership. The first is the one with which most people are familiar—you could be on the fifth floor of a building and you own only that airspace that your unit occupies.

The second is called a townhouse (technically known as a PUD, or planned unit development). Here, units are not arranged on top of one another. Rather, you own the ground underneath your unit and the airspace above.

TRAP

Don't make the mistake of thinking a townhouse is legally different from a condo. In terms of ownership, it's not. Rather, the difference is in the design. In a conventional condo, you only own an airspace. In a typical townhouse you own the ground underneath and the air above as well.

What Is a Co-op?

A co-op is a cooperatively owned property. This is different from condominium ownership. Here, as an individual, you don't actually own any separate airspace or ground. Rather, you own a share of stock in a company that owns the entire property. While you have the exclusive right to use a particular unit, you don't actually own it in the sense of being able to sell it directly. To sell your unit, you must sell your share in the company.

What Are the Pros and Cons of Condo versus Co-op Living?

It's important to understand the ownership difference between a condo and a co-op. With a condo you get title to the property; you actually own airspace (or in the case of a townhouse, the ground beneath and air above as well). You get a fee simple or absolute title.

With a co-op you do not get title to any real estate. Indeed, you do not own the real estate, the corporation does. With a co-op you get stock in the corporation that owns the real estate and that stock entitles you to a proprietary lease on a specified apartment from the corporation. You're a stockholder and a tenant, not a property owner.

While up until very recently, as noted earlier, condo owners were the last to take advantage of real estate boom periods, not so with many co-op owners. Most of the big gains occurred when an apartment building, located in an urban area (such as Manhattan), was converted to co-op status. The first to buy (often the former tenants) saw huge increases when they resold, in large part because of the shortage of available rentals. They bought an apartment in a city where just finding any place to live could be a problem.

Another factor has been timing. Most of the co-ops were established a good many years ago before the big price hikes in real estate that occurred in the late 1970s, the late 1980s, and once again in the late 1990s and, of course, early 2000s. If you bought prior to any of these market bumps, you would stand to see a big increase in value, regardless of the type of real estate. For those who bought co-ops in urban areas where there were already housing shortages (as noted above), the increases were even more dramatic.

On the other hand, there are some problems with co-op ownership not found with condos. First of all there are the finances. By its very nature a co-op tends to be less financially stable than a condo. Remember, when you buy into a condo, you own your unit. If you can't make the payments on your mortgage, you lose, not the other owners. (They only lose the fees that you would otherwise pay toward the upkeep of the common areas.)

With a co-op, however, an underlying mortgage is typically held by the corporation on the overall structure. That means that if you can't make your monthly payments to cover your portion of the mortgage debt, the other owners must make up what you can't pay in order to meet the monthly mortgage payment. The same holds true for property taxes and insurance. If too many owners can't pay, then the remainder might not be able to make up the difference and the entire project could conceivably go into foreclosure.

In short, with a co-op it is very much like an extended family with brothers, sisters, aunts, and uncles all living in close approximation and all contributing to the living expenses. When one (or more) loses a job or gets sick and can't contribute his or her share, the others must make it up. If they can't make it up, they could lose their home.

The inherent financial instability is the reason that good co-ops are very careful about whom they will allow to buy stock. They want to be sure that any new owners are financially strong.

TRAP

When buying into a co-op, expect to have a meeting before the Board in which you will have to show why you would be financially capable of being a good owner. While financial discrimination is allowed, discrimination based on gender, race, ethnic background, most medical problems or other similar concerns is prohibited. Nonetheless, some Boards have discriminated. Thus buying, and later reselling, your unit is potentially made harder.

Further, in some parts of the country, such as west of the Mississippi, getting financing to buy a co-op can be difficult. Lenders are concerned about the financial structure noted above, and they are simply not as familiar with the financing as with condos.

What Are the Pros and Cons of Condo/Co-ops versus Single-Family Homes?

When you buy into a shared ownership property (either condo or co-op), you are actually trading off a portion of your privacy in exchange for other benefits such as guaranteed maintenance, architectural control, and amenities, such as a pool, spa, rec room, tennis courts, clubhouse, and occasional parties, that go along with condominium living.

Shared versus Private Ownership

Pros of Owning a Single-Family House

- You are generally "master of your domain"
- Increased privacy
- No monthly owner fees paid to the HOA or Board
- Strong price appreciation in good markets

Cons of Owning a Single-Family House

- Generally more expensive on an absolute cost basis
- Maintenance required
- Little architectural control

Pros of Owning a Condo/Co-op

- Little or no exterior maintenance or repair
- Amenities such as pool or clubhouse
- Strict architectural control
- Sometimes utilities and insurance are paid for by the HOA
- Recently stronger price appreciation in good markets
- Often more security

Cons of Owning a Condo/Co-op

- Little say about the exterior of your unit
- Noisier
- Generally smaller units than single-family homes
- In a natural disaster (earthquake, hurricane) you could lose everything—depending on the insurance policies
- Historically slower price appreciation

A shared property is often the choice of those who are looking for a first or retirement house. The shared living means others are around to help out, the financing is usually the same as for a single-family house, and sometimes you can get into a good location for less (although on a square footage basis, you may also be getting less). Many first-time buyers purchase a condo or co-op and then live in it a few years, building up their equities. When they sell, they have a small nest egg that they can then apply toward a house. Many retirees opt for a condo or co-op because they don't want to mow lawns anymore and are concerned about security.

TRAP

If you buy into a condo/co-op, expect to spend some time on the homeowner association (or board of directors) just for self-protection. If you don't, you'll find that the HOA or Board will always seem to be doing something that you consider ridiculous or that you don't like. If you're an owner, you'll want to be a part of decisions that affect your home and its value. On the other hand, be aware of HOA burnout. This comes after you've been a member of the Board for a year or two and found that you can't get done what you want to get done. Often, owners will get discouraged and will then sell their unit. If you're at least aware of this possibility, you may be less inclined to make such a drastic move when a stalemate does occur.

As an additional resource on this topic, check into my book *Tips and Traps When Buying a Condo, Co-op, or Townhouse*, Second Edition (McGraw-Hill, 2007).

Reading Seller's Disclosures and Home Inspections

In the past, the dictum "Let the buyer beware!" was the rule in house hunting. Today, however, consumerism has turned the tables. Today it's "Let the seller beware." Sellers in most areas of the country must present to you, the buyer, a disclosure statement presumably listing any and all faults with the house, often at the time you first see it or at least at the time you make a purchase offer. (In California, for example, you have three days to evaluate the disclosure statement. If you're given the disclosure after the seller has accepted your offer and you don't like what the seller discloses, you can back out of the deal during that time.)

Further, sellers now expect a buyer to insist on a professional home inspection. After all, it protects the seller, in many cases, even more than you! The reason is that while sellers may know some of the home's problems (such as a leaky roof or broken window), they may know next to nothing about others such as the house's heating system or its foundation.

How Do You Read the Disclosures?

Reading the seller's disclosure statement is sometimes simple. Many sellers don't disclose anything. They simply refuse to say that their home has any defects. Take such negative disclosures with a big grain of salt. Either the sellers simply don't know their home or they are concealing something. Very few homes have absolutely no defects.

On the other hand, sometimes the disclosures will have innocuous sounding statements such as, "A few cracks in the wall below the dining room window." Wall cracks can be nothing more than signs that a house is settling, as most houses will do over time. However, cracks below a window are more ominous—they may indicate a cracked foundation.

Whenever the sellers disclose something seemingly harmless, check it out yourself. Or have a good home inspector check it out for you. You want to be sure that the disclosure isn't hiding something far more ominous.

Finally, there are disclosures of very serious problems such as leaking roofs, cracked foundation, sagging or broken structure, mold, and on and on. When this is the case, get someone to give you a rock solid estimate of how much it will cost to fix, and negotiate to have the seller pay for the repairs. Or, if the acknowledged damage is very serious, simply back out of the deal. (Hopefully your inspection contingency in the purchase agreement gives you the right of approval. If you don't approve, you're out of the deal with your deposit back and no recriminations.)

What Should You Do about the Inspection?

First, ask (demand) to see any previous inspection reports. Sellers should keep and present to you any previous reports, including those they obtained when they purchased the home as well as any from previous buyers who didn't complete the purchase. These can reveal much.

For that reason, sellers are often glad to have an inspector's report to go along with their disclosure statement to give to you. It shows they have diligently made an effort to learn about problems and disclose them.

TRAP

Expect to pay for your home inspection, probably around $250 to $350. And usually the inspector wants to be paid in cash at the time the inspection is completed! Make sure to arrange for how you'll pay in advance so you don't get a nasty surprise.

When to Insist on a Home Inspection

The time to insist on a home inspection is when you make your initial offer. Write it into the sales agreement. Make sure that it's a contingency of the purchase.

Sellers are almost universally prepared to let you have a home inspection. But they won't let you tie up their property indefinitely. Typically they will limit your inspection contingency by insisting that it be completed and your approval given within a set time, often no more than 14 days. If you don't approve, the deal's off and the house is back on the market. Indeed, many sellers will insist that they be able to continue showing the house and to accept backup offers until you remove the inspection contingency.

Where Do You Find a Home Inspector?

Ask your real estate agent. Usually active agents know of one they can recommend. However, also be wary. Although it seldom happens, it might be that an agent recommends a particular inspector mainly because he or she has a track record of going easy on the property, thereby helping to make the deal go through.

Look on the Internet. There are several national organizations that can recommend inspectors. My personal favorite is www.nachi.org (National Association of Certified Home Inspectors). Others to consider are www.ashi.com (American Society of Home Inspectors) and www.nahi.org (National Association of Home Inspectors). Getting a recommendation doesn't guarantee competence, but it indicates the inspector has at least gone through the effort to join a national trade association and is probably making an effort to get additional education and training. Also, each of the national organizations has a "standards of practice" that details what an inspector should do for you on an inspection (as well as what is not covered). And most insist that their members follow their standards.

You May Get an Unlicensed Inspector

At this point home inspectors are not yet licensed in many states. That means that anyone—you, I, or the guy next door—may be able to hang out a shingle and be an inspector. That means it's up to you to be sure you're dealing with someone competent.

Check Out Your Inspector

Ask your future inspector for at least three referrals from past jobs. Then call those people. Hopefully, it will be at least six months or more since the inspection and they will have had an opportunity to see if something came up that wasn't initially discovered. Ask them if they would use the inspector again.

You may get some surprising answers.

Check the inspector's credentials: What qualifies him or her to be an inspector? Look for someone with a related degree and a broad building background such as a soils or structural engineer. Often retired county or city building inspectors make great choices.

Some former contractors make money on the side as inspectors. That's okay, but just because a person has a contractor's license doesn't mean he or she knows anything about a home inspection. A plumbing contractor, for example, may be able to do a great job checking out your sinks and toilets, but may know next to nothing about the wiring.

Should You Go Along on the Inspection?

It's the only way you can really learn what the home's problems are. An inspection is both oral and written. In the oral part, the inspector describes problems to you as you go through, under, and over the home. You can ask questions and can often get useful information on how to correct a problem as well as how much that correction will cost.

TIP

Be sure to hand the inspector a copy of the seller's disclosures and highlight anything that the seller has noted. Ask the inspector if he or she can check it out. Most will make an effort to do so.

A written report, on the other hand, is often more formal. These days many inspectors are afraid to write down any but the most glaring problems for fear that they could be sued by the seller for exaggerating something. Hence, the written reports tend to be bland and, quite frankly, not all that useful. Often they are filled with more disclaimers than information. That's why you need to go along and listen to what the inspector says. Often, in casual conversation you'll learn far more than from the later written report.

What to Look For in a Home Inspection

Here are just a few warning signs (there are many others) in a house that you can watch out for and ask the inspector about during an inspection:

Warning Signs of Bad Defects

- **"V" shaped cracks in the foundation:** indicates serious cracking
- **Offsetting cracks in the foundation:** indicates serious cracking
- **Cracks in interior walls:** suggests structural problems, bad foundation
- **Water marks on the ceiling or roof rafters:** indicates a leaking roof
- **Water marks on basement walls:** indicates seasonal flooding
- **Standing water under home:** indicates poor drainage, possible foundation problems to come
- **Slanted floors:** suggests bad foundation or structural damage

The inspector will point things out. But your inspector might not be the best in the world, so you should have an idea what to look for yourself. Below is a home inspection checklist. Use it as a guide either with an inspector or, if you're bolder, when you inspect the property yourself. Keep in mind that while it offers many ideas, it is not complete. There may be problems with the property beyond the scope of the checklist.

TRAP

Don't try doing an inspection on your own unless you know a great deal about buildings, construction, and soils. I've been inspecting my own properties for more than 30 years and I still always hire a professional inspector to go along with me. The inspector can point out things that I miss . . . and vice versa.

Either when doing your own inspection or when accompanying a professional, here's a checklist of many of the things you'll want to look for.

Home Inspection Checklist

Drainage

Drainage problems can lead to cracked foundations and slabs. They can cause a house to shift, particularly if it's located on a hillside, and in extreme cases can cause the actual collapse of the home. The correction of drainage problems is best left to experts. However, even a beginner can usually tell where severe drainage problems exist.

Drainage Checklist

	YES	NO
• Is there dampness under the house? (The basement should be dry as dust.)	[ ]	[ ]
• Are there footprints or ribbed patterns in the dirt under the house, indicating that when it rains, water creeps in?	[ ]	[ ]

- Is there mold (black or green) on wood under the house, indicating heavy moisture? (There's almost a hysteria these days about black mold—check with your agent.) [ ] [ ]
- Does the ground outside slope *away* from the house? (If it slopes into the house, you've got serious problems.) [ ] [ ]

Foundation

The concrete foundation is what supports your house. Usually there is a peripheral foundation that goes around the entire edge of the home. Within this peripheral foundation there may be concrete blocks holding up piers that support the floor (in a wood floor home) or a concrete slab (in a cement floor home). The peripheral foundation typically has "footings" that extend downward perhaps two feet or more. (In freezing climates the footings should be below the freeze line.)

The further down the foundation extends and the wider it is, the better. In areas with expansive soil (the soil swells when wet) or other soil problems, the concrete foundation should be deep and wide enough to survive any expansion of the soil. In addition, there should be steel rods ("rebars" or reinforcement bars) in the concrete. The steel holds the concrete together. (Cement by itself, even with the new plasticizers and fibers, will tend to crack.)

Cracks in the foundation can lead to uneven floors inside the house. It can also lead to slippage down a hillside as well as to broken windows and cracks appearing in walls and ceilings. Some breakage of foundations happens naturally over time. However, severe breakage indicates a problem which could get worse.

Foundation Checklist

	YES	NO
• Do you see cracks in the foundation when you walk around the exterior of the house? (Hairline cracks always occur and usually can be disregarded.)	[ ]	[ ]
• Are the cracks wider at the top than at the bottom? (This indicates actual breakage, a serious problem.)	[ ]	[ ]
• Is there an actual separation in the foundation? (This indicates that not enough steel reinforcement was used when the foundation was built.)	[ ]	[ ]
• In a slab house, does the floor feel uneven when you walk over it (indicating cracks hidden under carpets or tiles)?	[ ]	[ ]
• Under a house, do any of the girders sag (a sign that the foundation has slipped)?	[ ]	[ ]

Roof

The cost of repairing a roof can be high, of replacing a roof enormous ($5,000 to $25,000 or more depending on the materials used). You want to be sure that the roof is in good shape. If it's not, you may want to have the seller fix or replace it or make an adjustment to the price.

Wood Shake Roof. Depending on the thickness of the shake, it can last 20 to 30 years. If the house you are buying has a wood shake roof and it's 20 years old or older, check the roof very carefully.

Wood Shake Roof Checklist

	YES	NO
• Are there pieces of the roof lying on the ground around the house? (This is an obvious bad sign.)	[ ]	[ ]
• Using binoculars (don't walk on the roof itself—you might damage the roof, or fall off!), can you see missing shingles anywhere on the roof?	[ ]	[ ]
• Are the shingles intact? (Badly cracked shingles are another bad sign.)	[ ]	[ ]
• Are there any signs of leakage in the ceiling or walls inside the house? Go into the attic and look up. If it's daytime and you see light pouring through many tiny or large holes, you've got trouble.	[ ]	[ ]

Composition Shingle Roof. Made of tar, fiberglass, or some similar composition, it has a lifespan of 15 to 30 years, depending on the quality and materials.

Composition Shingle Roof Checklist

	YES	NO
• Is the *color* of the shingles good? (Fading shingles are a sign of wear.)	[ ]	[ ]
• Are the edges of the shingles curling up? (This is a sign of wear in hot climates.)	[ ]	[ ]
• Are there any bare spots on the roof?	[ ]	[ ]
• Are there any signs of leakage in the ceiling or walls inside the house?	[ ]	[ ]

Aluminum Shingle Roof. This type of roof has a lifespan of 50 years or so. Generally it doesn't wear out unless it has been damaged.

Aluminum Shingle Roof Checklist

	YES	NO
• Are there signs of peeling or fading of their color? The shingles may continue to keep the weather out, but will look terrible.)	[ ]	[ ]
• Are there any dents or separations in the shingles, indicating someone has walked on them?	[ ]	[ ]
• Are there any signs of leakage in the ceiling or walls inside the house?	[ ]	[ ]

Tile Shingle Roof. A tile roof lasts indefinitely (80 years or more). However, it can easily be broken, and once broken it quickly loses its ability to keep the weather out. *Don't walk on tile roofs—you'll break the tiles.*

Tile Shingle Roof Checklist

	YES	NO
• Are any of the tiles broken?	[ ]	[ ]
• Have any fallen off?	[ ]	[ ]
• Are there any signs of leakage in the ceiling or walls inside the house?	[ ]	[ ]

Paint

Interior. In a resale, don't expect to get a house that doesn't require repainting. As soon as the seller's furniture gets moved out, you're going to see whole areas that need repainting. The only question is: Will you do it or will the seller?

Interior Paint Checklist

	YES	NO
• Are there marks on the walls?	[ ]	[ ]
• Is the current paint flaking, indicating it will have to be sanded before new paint can be applied?	[ ]	[ ]
• Are the colors light or dark? (Covering dark colors may require two or more new coats.)	[ ]	[ ]
• Is there lead in the paint? (You may want to have it tested. Homes painted prior to 1978, when lead was banned from paint, often have lead paint in them. Your agent should be able to suggest a lead testing company nearby or check with www.epa.gov. The sellers are also required to give you a lead paint disclosure.)	[ ]	[ ]

Exterior.   Weathering is the problem here. Even the best paints usually don't last more than five to seven years. Repainting the exterior can be more expensive than painting the interior, since it often requires removing chipped and peeling paint.

Exterior Paint Checklist

	YES	NO
• Is the paint chipped or peeling?	[ ]	[ ]
• Are the colors faded? (Faded colors indicate paint that is aging.)	[ ]	[ ]
• Is the caulking around windows starting to fall out?	[ ]	[ ]
• Is the paint on the gutters or siding peeling?	[ ]	[ ]

Plumbing

In general, you need an expert to tell you if there are serious plumbing problems. There are, however, some telltale signs you can check for.

Plumbing Checklist

	YES	NO
• Is the plumbing galvanized steel? (Galvanized steel lasts about 30 years, sometimes less. Copper lasts virtually forever.)	[ ]	[ ]
• Are there leaks as indicated by rust marks at the joints of galvanized pipes? (Usually visible under the house or in the garage, leaks indicate that electrolytic action may be corroding the pipes and they could need to be replaced—$5,000 to $10,000 or more for the whole house.)	[ ]	[ ]
• Are there leaks under the sinks in any of the bathrooms or kitchen? [Possibly a minor problem, but why should you (and not the seller) have to fix it?]	[ ]	[ ]
• Is the water heater old? (The date is sometimes stamped on the label—a water heater rarely lasts more than 7 to 10 years in areas with silt in the water or high electrolytic action.)	[ ]	[ ]
• Does the water heater have a temperature/ pressure safety valve? (This is vitally important. If you're not sure what a safety valve is, have a professional check it out.)	[ ]	[ ]

In addition, the gas supply line needs to be checked. A professional should do this.

Wiring

This is the venue of the professional. Don't attempt to make a judgment on the wiring unless you're an electrician. Some danger signals to watch for include switches or sockets that spark when used and inoperative lights or switches. **Never attempt to check any electrical item unless the power is completely off!**

Heating

Even more so than in the case of wiring, a professional needs to check out the heating. If you're using gas, you need to be sure that there are no leaks. Some telltale signs to look for include smelling burned gas fumes coming from heating vents and yellow flames in the furnace that rise above the burners. These are bad signs indicating a leak in the heat exchanger, a dangerous condition usually requiring replacement of the furnace—$3,500 or more. Also, if you smell gas (a sulfurous odor) around the furnace, it's a very dangerous sign—ask the seller to call the gas company immediately.

Fireplace

Most people figure that there's little to go wrong with a fireplace. Unfortunately, that's not the case. The bricks in a fireplace can crack and the fireplace itself can pull away from the house (something which happens all too often in earthquake country). Even more serious, the interior casing can break allowing dangerous gasses to enter the house. A bad fireplace is a dangerous situation which can lead to house fires, poisoning, or asphyxiation. *Have a professional check it out.*

Fireplace Checklist

	YES	NO
• From the outside, is there a separation between the fireplace and the house? (A separation is a big danger sign.)	[ ]	[ ]
• Are there any visible cracks in the external bricks of the fireplace?	[ ]	[ ]
• Are there any cracks in the firebricks inside the fireplace?	[ ]	[ ]
• Does the flue work?	[ ]	[ ]
• Does the fireplace draw properly—no smoke getting into the house?	[ ]	[ ]

Tile

Tile problems are usually easily spotted since they consist mostly of cracks in the tiles or staining of the grout.

Tile Checklist

	YES	NO
• Are there any cracks in the tile of the kitchen or bathrooms? (Cracks can simply be caused by dropping something heavy on the tile, or they can be symptomatic of broken cabinets, house movements, or even a cracked foundation.)	[ ]	[ ]
• Are floor tiles cracked? (Replacing cracked floor tiles when there is a problem with the floor simply means that the replacement tiles will soon crack too. Fixing the underlying floor problem could be very expensive.)	[ ]	[ ]

What Do You Do with the Termite Report?

When you get a new loan, the lender almost always requires a termite clearance. This is a report from a registered termite company that states that the house is free of infestation.

It's important to understand that the report is of limited value. In areas where termites are endemic, there will almost always be some infestation. (The report usually states the house to be clear of termites for 60 to 180 days—the inspectors know that after that the termites likely will be back.)

In order to get a clearance, repair work often must be done. In some cases this is minor, involving the replacement of some wood and occasionally spraying. In other cases it is major, requiring the tenting and poisonous gassing of the house. Modern techniques may involve freezing the termites out of localized areas.

In most cases the termites chomp away at the wood structure of the home and are of little consequence. The real problem is that over 30 or 40 years, they can eat enough of the wood to make the house unstable or, in very severe cases, actually collapse.

Usually the seller will pay for any corrective work. You, however, will likely be responsible for any preventative work, but that is at your option. (You usually aren't required to do it.)

What About Environmental Hazards?

Thus far we've been dealing with typical problems that you can look for in any home. There are, however, additional problems which may be of a hazardous nature. You should be aware of these and have a professional check for them.

Also, certain parts of the country are now requiring buyer and seller to sign off on some of these problems as well as other potential hazards. Be sure to check with your real estate agent about any conditions on the sale that the city, county, or state may impose. Additionally there may be federal requirements, as is the case with lead.

Asbestos Ceilings

Prior to about 1980, blown-in ceilings sometimes contained asbestos fibers. If you're worried about them, these ceilings may have to be scraped and removed or encapsulated with a sealant and a nonasbestos mixture. The cost for this can be high. To find out, you need to have your ceiling professionally tested.

Wrapped Asbestos Pipes

In some parts of the country, heating pipes under the house or in the basement were wrapped in asbestos insulation. If undisturbed and sealed, there is usually little problem. If the seal is damaged or disturbed, it may need to be removed by experts and the pipes rewrapped. You need to have all work done professionally.

Leaded Copper Pipe Joints

Prior to about 1986, the solder used to connect copper pipes in houses was made of a mixture of tin and lead. It was discovered that the lead would sometimes leach into water that sat in the pipes. (Modern solders use a nonlead mixture.) There is little that can be done about this short of resoldering all the copper joints. However, after about five years the leaching process tends to become minimal. It's mostly a problem in houses that are less than five years old. (You can run the water a while before using it to reduce the risk of lead poisoning.)

Smoke Alarms

These should be installed on all floors and near kitchens and fireplaces as well as in every bedroom.

Insulation

This isn't really a hazard. However, if you're in cold country without adequate insulation, you can be mighty uncomfortable. Adding new insulation to an older home can be a problem. While roof insulation usually can easily be blown into an attic space, for walls, it's much more difficult. In some areas, holes were cut and a formaldehyde-based insulation shot into the walls. However, formaldehyde itself is a health hazard and where this has been done, sometimes the walls must be cut open and the insulation removed. Check with a good insulation company in your area regarding your options.

Earthquake Retrofitting

In some parts of the country, particularly the West Coast, new laws are being proposed and are coming on line that may eventually require sellers to retrofit older homes and bring them up to earthquake safety standards.

This may be something as simple as tying the framing down to the foundation or as complex as putting steel reinforcements from the foundation up to the roof. Be sure to check out what's necessary in your area and have the seller do the expensive work.

Flood Plain

Some homes are built on a flood plain. It may not flood more than once every 50 or 100 years. But if you're the owner during that year, you lose. Often insurance is hard to get and expensive. Check it out.

Radon Gas Hazard

Radon is a naturally occurring gas in many soils. In some areas it can leak out of the ground and accumulate in the basement and, sometimes, in other areas of a house. It is a health hazard.

This is something that should be checked, particularly if you are in an area where radon gas leakage is common. Simple testing kits are available for under $50.

If radon gas is a problem, an environmental engineer should be contacted to determine how it can be eliminated from the home. Often increasing the ventilation in a basement will do the trick.

Other times expensive electronic venting systems are needed. In a very few cases, it may be impossible to eliminate the hazard, in which case you may want to look elsewhere.

Lead Paint Hazard

If the house you are considering was built before the late 1970s (when lead paint was banned), chances are lead paint was used both inside and out. Lead is a serious health threat. It can produce sickness, retardation, and, in extreme cases, even death. The most common means of getting lead poisoning is when children chew on molding or other painted areas of a house and ingest the lead paint.

Sometimes old exterior paint containing lead will flake or dust off and contaminate the ground around the outside of the house where children play, and they may ingest some of the soil. By federal mandate, the seller must present you with a disclosure statement and pamphlet regarding this hazard. (However, this statement often simply says that the seller is unaware of the lead hazard in the property, throwing it back in your court.)

Safely removing lead paint is difficult and requires a qualified specialist. It can easily cost $10,000 or more to remove it properly from a home. On the other hand, people sometimes incorrectly paint over the lead paint with a nontoxic modern paint and hope for the best. (Encapsulation is *not* considered an approved method of dealing with lead paint.) Few sellers are willing to pop for the cost of removing lead paint.

Thus the choice becomes yours—are you willing to live in a house with this hazard? Many buyers of older homes who are made aware of the lead paint problem through the disclosure statement do move forward with the deal but vow to watch their children more closely. If this problem bothers you, opt for a newer home.

Black Mold

This is the hazard de jour in many areas. Black mold has been around since time immemorial. However, some have suggested that a new more toxic variety is now attacking houses. Thus the CDC (Centers for Disease Control) and many state environmental agencies are conducting studies to see if black mold poses a serious health hazard. Certainly some people are allergic to molds and this poses a health problem to them. I have even heard reports of people dying from a certain variety of black mold. The more basic problem is that a kind of hysteria has surrounded homes that contain black mold. Many buyers will shy away from contaminated houses, meaning that if you buy a house containing black mold, even if you're not concerned about yourself, you may have trouble reselling it later on.

This is a serious problem because most homes in wet climates tend to have it. Therefore, you should have the house checked for black mold. Finding serious black mold should weigh heavily into your purchase decision.

Having your home professionally inspected is an important part of the purchase process. Don't skimp on it. Use a good professional.

How to Turn Your Credit Around

oday, being credit challenged does not necessarily mean you can't get real estate financing. There is undoubtedly a lender out there somewhere for everyone, even if that lender is the seller. However, the worse your credit usually the higher the interest rate, the lower the LTV (loan-to-value—ratio of the loan to the value of the property), and the fewer properties available to you. All of which is to say, if you have credit problems, your ability to afford the home of your dreams is greatly diminished.

Before trying to buy a home, it's a good idea to check out your credit. These days, it's easy to do. You can go online to www.freeannualcreditreport.com where once a year you can get a free credit report from each of the three national credit bureaus. You can also contact each of these directly for a credit report on yourself (usually for a nominal fee).

The three major credit reporting agencies are:

Equifax   www.equifax.com
Experian   www.experian.com
TransUnion   www.transunion.com

There are some legitimate ways to improve your credit. Here are 12 suggestions that should help both in the long term and in the short run.

1. Change Your Attitude

Many people are surprised to learn that even a few late payments can seriously affect their ability to get real estate financing. The attitude toward bills, "I'll pay when I'm good and ready," may sound defiant against a creditor whom you dislike, but when those late payments show up on your credit report, your future mortgage lender wonders if you'll say the same thing to it?

If you're behind in payments, catch up *before* applying for the mortgage. Try to stay caught up for at least one year before applying so your delinquencies will show up as old rather than recent. Old delinquencies are much easier to forgive.

2. Verify Your Credit

As noted above, check with the three national credit bureaus: Experian, TransUnion, and Equifax. They contain input from many other smaller credit-reporting agencies around the country. If you've paid your bills on time, that will show up on this report. And if you haven't paid bills on time and have other problems, they will show up as well. Mortgage lenders regularly order a "3-bureau" report that sends them your credit from all three. Which is to say you can't hide bad credit.

If you find that there are errors, correct them. The credit bureaus will tell you how. If there are problems, see if they can be fixed (see below).

3. Check Your FICO Score

FICO stands for Fair Isaac and is an independent company that evaluates credit reports by assigning the borrower a numerical rating between 350 and 850. Virtually all lenders use the FICO score. Typically, if you score in the mid–700s, or higher, you'll get financing. Score 800 or higher and you'll get the best financing. Score lower than about 700 and the financing becomes problematic. You can check your FICO score online at www.myfico.com as well as get useful hints on improving it.

Factors Affecting Your FICO Score

- Timely repayment of debt (deduct for slow/no payments)
- Foreclosures/bankruptcies (deduct big)
- How much you currently owe (The less the better in relation to how much credit you have. No more than 50 percent on any credit line is good.)
- Your recent applications for credit (more than three in the last six months could be trouble)
- How long you've had your credit cards (the longer—over 10 years—the better)
- Your money management (your history of borrowing wisely)

4. Improve Your Income/Expense Ratio

You shouldn't fudge, but how you express your income can make a difference. When filling out a mortgage application it usually pays to emphasize length and continuity. For example, you're a teacher who has gotten his first job in years just a month ago. The lender is bound to wonder if you will succeed at the work. However, if you note that you were a teacher with nine years' experience a decade ago before leaving the field to help raise children, it can help put your application in a whole new and better light. The lender may be inclined to now count all of your new income instead of just a portion of it.

5. If You Are Self-Employed, Try Low-Doc Loans

The method in which you receive your income is important too. If you work for an employer and receive wages (meaning a W-2 form at the end of the year), you get preference, mainly because it is easy to verify your income and because, presumably, you have something called "job security."

On the other hand, if you're self-employed, you may be turned down. Usually, at minimum you will be asked to produce the last two years of 1040 tax forms. However, in some cases of self-employed individuals this may not tell the whole story because you have cash income "off the books." Another problem is if you have been in business for less than two years.

In these cases, ask a mortgage broker about low-documentation mortgages. They don't require as much proof of your income as is the case with normal mortgages.

TRAP

Up until recently, many lenders would allow "no-doc" loans where you simply stated your income without documentation. After the credit crunch of 2008, however, these have become virtually nonexistent.

Recently low-doc loans have been coming back slowly. If you can find a lender who offers one, you may be able to get the loan based on factors such as just your veracity, money in your account, bank recommendations, and so on.

6. Pay Off Excess Debt

In calculating how big a monthly payment/mortgage to give you, lenders take into account your available income. However, the more debt you currently have, the less income is available to pay the new mortgage. Therefore, when possible, pay off as much of your short-term (such as from credit cards) debt as possible. That way you increase your income (less is set aside to pay for the short-term debt) and you may have a better chance of qualifying.

There is a downside to this, however. The more debt you pay off, the less cash you'll have available for a down payment and closing costs. It's really a balancing act.

7. Put More Money Down

Whether or not you can get financing at a decent interest rate is determined in no small part by how much money you put down. If you have excellent credit, you might be able to get a mortgage with low down payment financing (10 percent down—5 percent down or nothing down is rare these days).

On the other hand, if your credit isn't wonderful, then in order to get a mortgage, you might have to put more cash down. It works similarly with the interest rate charged. Generally speaking, the greater your down payment, the lower an interest rate you're likely to get. (Not lower than market, but less of an added premium for a high-risk loan.) Put down 20 percent and most lenders will accept you. Put down 30 percent and lenders will love you!

8. Borrow Early for the Down Payment and Closing Costs

Ideally your down payment and closing costs will come from your own funds, earned over the years and set aside as savings. Borrowing the down payment can be a problem. Borrowing the down payment suggests to the lender that you really can't afford the property. Let the lender know you're borrowing your down payment and you almost certainly will be scuttling the loan.

Therefore, if you need to borrow money that you intend to use as part of the down payment, do it well in advance of applying for the mortgage (at least six months). That way the money will be seen as part of a savings account and the loan will be long established. In other words, you won't be borrowing specifically to make the home purchase.

Gifts for the down payment from relatives also may be acceptable. These must, however, be legitimate gifts. They can't be given with strings attached, such as you'll repay them so much a month and when you sell the property you'll repay the balance in full. In that case they are nothing more than a disguised loan.

9. Hang On to Old Credit Card Accounts

Lenders want to know that you've been successfully borrowing for a long time. That tells them that you're a good money manager. To determine this they look at your oldest trade lines (credit cards). The older the better.

I've had credit cards for over 20 years. When I recently applied for credit, it was noted that I didn't have long-term cards. Long term meant 30 years or more! Hang on to your old credit cards. Keep a credit card that you've had for years, even if a new credit company offers you a somewhat better deal. That old credit card shows that you have a long history and may help you get your mortgage. This is the case even if you just keep the card in a box and almost never use it!

10. Don't Have Too Much Credit

Generally speaking, if you apply for credit more than three times within a six month period, it's likely to be a mark against you. (Yes, it's irrational reasoning!) To a lender it looks suspiciously like you may be planning to borrow a lot of money and leave the country.

A good balance between credit cards, car loans, personal finance companies, and other installment loans is best. You don't want a lot of any of these or even a huge total. But the fact that you've got a car loan, three credit cards (a good number), and perhaps a department store card, and you've maintained reasonable balances all suggest you're a good credit manager. And that's what the lenders actually want the most.

By the way, don't go to the limit in your credit card charges. It's probably better if you owe half your limit on two cards, than go to your entire limit on one.

11. Get Bad Credit Fixed

It's a mistaken belief that you can have all bad credit "fixed." Companies that offer to fix or make any credit problem simply disappear, particularly if they charge you a hefty fee for doing it, may be nothing more than scams.

On the other hand, some types of bad credit can be remedied, either by doing it yourself or by hiring a company to do it for you. Some of the bad credit that can be fixed includes:

Fixable Bad Credit

- The wrong name, address, Social Security number, and/or employer
- A creditor's error in reporting a late payment that you made or a continuing loan that you paid off
- A foreclosure that didn't occur or a bankruptcy that never happened

You get the idea. Mistakes and errors can be corrected. But it often takes time and effort to do so.

12. Explain a Problem

If you have a credit problem that can't be fixed, give a logical and coherent explanation for it. If your explanation shows that you at least tried to solve the problem and, perhaps even more important, that the problem was isolated and isn't likely to happen again, you may very well be able to get the financing you want.

The best way to do this is to be up front with the lender. Don't wait for the problem to surface as part of your credit report. Get it out in the open. And provide the lender with a clearly written letter of explanation. If you have late payments because you were ill, but are now well, tell that to the lender. If you were out of work, but have now been employed steadily for a year or more and are paying back your credit problems, explain it. If you had a foreclosure, explain how it occurred and why circumstances are different now.

No, an explanation won't eliminate bad credit. But some lenders will listen to reason and give you the benefit of the doubt.

A Financing Primer

Let's face it, we live in a credit society. A family with a $100,000 annual income can easily obtain a new car loan with almost nothing down and a $500-a-month car payment. But that same family may not have $500 in the bank in a savings account. In fact, over 50 percent of all families have little or no cash savings. (On the other hand, 30 percent or so have whopping big savings accounts!)

I'm reminded of that old saw about the two investors who want to buy the Empire State Building in New York. The first investor, just returned from a meeting with the sellers, tells the second, "I've got good news and bad. The good news is that they'll take our $100 million offer." "Great," says the second investor. "What's the bad news?" "They want $500 cash down!"

Where Do You Find a Good Lender?

For a real estate mortgage, you can go to a single source lender such as your bank or your credit union. Or a multiple source lender such as a mortgage broker.

The mortgage broker has the advantage because he or she solicits loans from a wide variety of lenders including banks, insurance companies, and pools of investors. Often a mortgage broker can match you up with just the right lender for your needs.

Ask your real estate agent for a mortgage broker recommendation. Also, check with any friends, relatives, or associates who recently bought a home. Chances are they used a mortgage broker and can recommend (or steer you away from!) a mortgage broker. As a last resort they are listed in the yellow pages under Mortgage Brokers. (Note a mortgage *banker* may not make loans directly to consumers. Look for a mortgage *broker*.)

Also, consider online mortgage brokers. Check a good search engine for them. Also, look into:

E-Loan, Inc.	www.eloan.com
Quicken	www.quicken.com
LendingTree	www.lendingtree.com

Will a Lender Give You 100 Percent of the Purchase Price?

The "standard" down payment on a home 20 years ago was 20 percent. That's $40,000 on a $200,000 property, a lot of money for most people.

During the real estate bubble, you could easily get financing for 90 percent of your purchase. Depending on your financial situation, you were able to get 100 percent, sometimes even 103 percent of financing (to help pay for some of your closing costs)! These were mostly "conforming" loans. (They conformed to Fannie Mae and Freddie Mac underwriting standards.)

More recently, financing has gone backward a bit. Bigger down payments are now the rule, typically around 10 to 20 percent down.

Low-Down Mortgages for Low-Income Earners

There are ways to get financing with little to nothing down for low-income families. Both Fannie Mae and Freddie Mac offer these as do the VA (Department of Veterans Affairs) and the FHA (Federal Housing Administration). Again, check with a good mortgage broker.

What Is Mortgage Insurance?

All FHA loans have it. And all conforming loans where the loan amount is greater than 80 percent normally require it. In other words, on a $100,000 house, if you put less than 20 percent down, you're probably stuck with paying private mortgage insurance (PMI).

Mortgage insurance does not protect you. It protects the lender. If you don't make your payments and the lender has to foreclose on you, the insurance picks up a substantial portion of any loss the lender may incur. That's why lenders demand it. (That and the fact that the government requires it!)

PMI is expensive. Expect to pay an additional $1/4$ to $3/4$ percent in interest for it. However, once you pay your loan down (or your property appreciates) so that your mortgage is less than 80 percent of the value of your property, you can usually get it removed.

Be Creative—Have the Seller Handle the Financing for You

What used to be called "creative financing" is nothing more than having the seller finance your purchase. Here, instead of going to an institution, such as a bank, to get a mortgage, the seller carries back the "paper," sometimes for the entire price.

However, in order for the seller to do this, he or she must have a substantial equity in the property. Often this is the case with retirees who are downsizing. They want to get a smaller home and often have their existing home paid off, or close to it.

While they may need some cash, often they come out of the sale with a lot of extra money, which they then put into the bank or CDs to earn interest. However, if interest rates are low, they are in for a hard time getting a good return on their funds, until you suggest borrowing money from them as part of the purchase. While the bank may pay them only a few percentage points in interest, they can easily get much more from you. For a seller who is looking for income rather than cash, you can be a godsend.

Often these seller-financed sales are constructed with two mortgages. You go out and get a conventional first mortgage for up to 80 percent of the sales price. (These are obtainable with decent credit and income.) Then the seller lends you an additional 10 to 20 percent to cover what otherwise would be your down payment. If you can't get an 80 percent institutional loan, you may be able to get a 70 percent one with the seller carrying back up to 30 percent.

Pluses of Seller Financing

- It's almost instantaneous—There's no waiting for a lender to fund.
- Little qualifying—Most sellers only want to see a credit report showing relatively good credit.

- High LTVs (Loan-to-Value)—Often a seller will give you the top 10 to 30 percent that would otherwise be your down payment.

Minuses of Seller Financing

- Sometimes it's hard to find a seller with enough equity who doesn't need to cash out (to buy another property).
- Sellers may be wary—If you don't make the payments, they would need to foreclose, and their lack of experience and knowledge makes that difficult.

Some Sellers Are Wary

Some of the "no money down" craze that was popularized in real estate a few years ago involved having sellers carry back all the down payment—20 percent or sometimes even more. The sellers were placed at a real disadvantage in terms of collateral. When some buyers defaulted, the sellers had to foreclose, often to ruined properties and financial losses.

As a result, having heard of this past ill treatment, today's sellers are often wary of buyers suggesting seller financing. To gain a seller's confidence you may have to offer a bigger down payment (meaning putting up more cash) and produce a better credit report/score.

Other Sources for the Down Payment

It would be nice if we could simply write out a check for the down payment if we can't get 100 percent financing. However, most of us are always pressed for cash. Other than a flush checking or savings account, here are some sources of cash for a down payment which you may not have considered before.

Alternative Possible Sources of Down Payment*

- Cash value of life insurance (borrowing on it)
- Refinancing or selling an auto or boat
- Sale of other physical assets to generate cash
- Sale of stocks, bonds, or other securities
- Sale of present home
- Gifts or loans from relatives or friends
- Refinancing investment real estate you already own (should be obtained before applying for the loan)
- Income tax refund
- Letter of credit or credit line from a bank (should be obtained before applying for the loan)
- MasterCard, Visa, or other credit card (should be obtained before applying for the loan)
- "Sweat equity"—offering to fix up a house in return for a reduced down payment
- Accumulation of funds from your regular income between date of purchase and close of escrow (insist on a long escrow—three months or more)
- Personal loan on hobby materials, jewelry or furs, cameras, or other property

Beware When Borrowing the Down Payment

Many of the sources of cash listed above involve borrowing. However, many loan programs restrict the borrowing of funds for a down payment. (Not all—some Fannie Mae and Freddie Mac programs specifically allow it.) Be sure to check with what your lender

---

* Check with your accountant before cashing in your life insurance or dipping into any retirement account. You may need to preserve these funds for retirement or other uses.

requires. If you do borrow your down payment, it's a good idea to borrow it at least six months before you enter into a transaction to purchase a home. That way, you'll have the cash in hand and borrowing will show up as an existing loan against your credit, not new borrowing, which could disqualify you.

It's important to be aware that an extra loan against your credit could decrease the amount you could borrow on a home. (You will be tying up some of your income to pay off that loan. That income won't be available to help you qualify for a home mortgage.)

Don't Overlook the Closing Costs

Many buyers simply forget about this very real cost. Don't. Closing costs are expensive. Typically they are around 5 to 8 percent of the purchase price of the house. If you pay $100,000 for a home, expect to pay about $5,000 to $8,000 in closing costs.

These are cash costs. You'll need to come up with money to pay them *in addition* to your down payment. Reread Chapter 10 if you're not sure what they involve.

Reducing or Eliminating the Closing Costs

It's possible to get your closing costs reduced, eliminated, or deferred. One method is to have your mortgage amount increased to cover the closing costs. You are getting a $100,000 mortgage with $5,000 in closing costs. This is converted to a $105,000 mortgage with no closing costs. Check with your lender to see if it can be done.

Another option is to have the lender roll the closing costs into the loan. You end up with a slightly higher interest rate (around $3/8$ percent more), but the lender covers your closing costs. You are getting a $100,000 mortgage with $5,000 in closing costs at

6 percent interest. This is converted to a $100,000 mortgage with no closing costs at $6\frac{3}{8}$ percent. Again, check with a lender.

Yet another option is to negotiate the closing costs with the seller before you commit to the purchase. Remember, closing costs are negotiable. You and the seller can agree between yourselves who will pay them. As part of the deal, the seller can agree to pay all or part of your closing costs for you.

Why Would a Seller Pay Your Costs?

What are the chances of a seller agreeing to pay your closing costs? Pretty good in a buyer's market where the seller is desperate to unload a house. Not so good in a seller's market where houses are moving rapidly. Also, keep in mind that negotiability extends to all areas of the transaction. If you're getting a terrific price, the seller is less inclined to pay part or all of your closing costs. On the other hand, if you're giving the seller pretty much what he or she wants in price and the market isn't too tight, then reduced closing costs may be possible.

In today's market, getting financing is the key to making a home purchase. Get your financing ducks in a row before you begin looking for a property, and you'll find doors opening for you when it comes time to make an offer.

Understanding Real Estate Talk

I f you're just getting introduced to real estate, you'll quickly realize that people in this field have a language all their own. There are points and disclosures and contingencies and dozens of other terms that can make you think people are talking in a foreign language.

Since buying a home is one of the biggest financial decisions in life, it's a good idea to become familiar with the following terms, which are frequently used in real estate. All too often a lack of understanding can result in very real consequences such as confusion and failure to act (or inappropriate action) on an important issue.

Abstract of Title.   A written document produced by a title insurance company (in some states an attorney will do it) giving the history of who owned the property from the first owner forward. It also indicates any liens or encumbrances that may affect the title.

A lender will not make a loan, nor can a sale normally conclude, until the title to real estate is clear, as evidenced by the abstract.

Acceleration Clause. A clause that "accelerates" the payments in a mortgage, meaning that the entire amount becomes immediately due and payable. Most mortgages contain this clause (which kicks in if, for example, you sell the property).

Adjustable-Rate Mortgage (ARM). A mortgage whose interest rate fluctuates according to an index and a margin agreed to in advance by borrower and lender.

Adjustment Date. The day on which an adjustment is made in an adjustable-rate mortgage. It may occur monthly, every six months, once a year, or as otherwise agreed.

Agent. Any person licensed to sell real estate, whether a broker or a salesperson.

Alienation Clause. A clause in a mortgage specifying that if the property is transferred to another person, the mortgage becomes immediately due and payable. See also Acceleration Clause.

ALTA (American Land Title Association). A more complete and extensive policy of title insurance and one that most lenders insist upon. It involves a physical inspection and often guarantees the property's boundaries. Lenders often insist on an ALTA policy, with themselves named as beneficiary.

Amortization. Paying back the mortgage in equal installments. In other words, if the mortgage is for 30 years, you pay in 360 equal installments. (The last payment is often a few dollars more or less. This is the opposite of a Balloon Payment, which is a payment that is considerably larger than the rest.) See Balloon Payment.

Annual Percentage Rate (APR).   The rate paid for a loan, including interest, loan fees, and points as determined by a government formula.

Appraisal.   Valuation of a property, usually by a qualified appraiser, as required by most lenders. The amount of the appraisal is the maximum value on which the loan will be based. For example, if the appraisal is $100,000 and the lender loans 80 percent of value, the maximum mortgage will be $80,000.

As Is.   A property sold without warrantees from the sellers. The sellers are essentially saying that they won't make any repairs.

ASA (American Society of Appraisers).   A professional organization of appraisers.

Assignment of Mortgage.   The lender's sale of a mortgage usually without the borrower's permission. For example, you may obtain a mortgage from XYZ Savings and Loan, which then sells the mortgage to Bland Bank. You will get a letter saying that the mortgage was assigned and you are to make your payments to a new entity. The document used between lenders for the transfer is the "assignment of mortgage."

Assumption.   Taking over an existing mortgage. For example, a seller may have an assumable mortgage on a property. When you buy the property, you take over that seller's obligation under the loan. Today most fixed-rate mortgages are not assumable.

Most adjustable-rate mortgages are assumable, but the borrower must qualify. FHA and VA mortgages may be assumable if certain conditions are met. When you assume the mortgage, you may be personally liable if there is a foreclosure.

Automatic Guarantee.   The power assigned to some lenders to guarantee VA loans without first checking with the Department of

Veterans Affairs. These lenders can often make the loans more quickly.

Backup.   An offer that comes in after an earlier offer is accepted. If both buyer and seller agree, the backup assumes a secondary position to be acted upon only if the original deal does not go through.

Balloon Payment.   A single mortgage payment, usually the last, that is larger than all the others. In the case of second mortgages held by sellers, often only interest is paid until the due date—then the entire amount borrowed (the principal) is due. See Second Mortgage.

Biweekly Mortgage.   A mortgage that is paid every other week instead of monthly. Since there are 52 weeks in the year, you end up making 26 payments, or the equivalent of one month's extra payment. The additional payments, applied to the principal, significantly reduce the amount of interest charged on the mortgage and often reduce the term of the loan.

Blanket Mortgage.   A mortgage that covers several properties instead of a single property. It is used most frequently by developers and builders.

Broker.   An independent licensed agent, one who can establish his or her own office. Salespeople, although they are licensed, must work for brokers, typically for a few years, to get enough experience to become licensed as brokers.

Buydown Mortgage.   A mortgage with a lower than market interest rate, either for the entire term of the mortgage or for a set period at the beginning—say, two years. The buydown is made possible by the builder or seller paying an up-front fee to the lender.

Buyer's Agent.   A real estate agent whose loyalty is to the buyer and not to the seller. Such agents are becoming increasingly common today.

Call Provision.   A clause in a mortgage allowing the lender to call in the entire unpaid balance of the loan providing certain events have occurred, such as sale of the property. See also Acceleration Clause.

Canvass.   To work a neighborhood, to go through it and knock on every door. Agents canvass to find listings. Investors and home buyers do it to find potential sellers who have not yet listed their property and may agree to sell quickly for less.

Caps.   Limits put on an adjustable-rate mortgage. The interest rate, the monthly payment, or both may be capped.

CC&Rs (covenants, conditions, and restrictions).   These limit the activities you as an owner may do. For example, you may be required to seek approval of a Homeowners Association before adding on or changing the color of your house. Or you may be restricted from adding a second or third story to your home.

Certificate of Reasonable Value (CRV).   A document issued by the Department of Veterans Affairs establishing what the VA feels is the property's maximum value. In some cases, if a buyer pays more than this amount for the property, he or she will not get the VA loan.

Chain of Title.   The history of ownership of the property. The title to property forms a chain going back to the first owners, which in the Southwest, for example, may come from original Spanish land grants.

Closing.   When the seller conveys title to the buyer and the buyer makes full payment, including financing, for the property. At the closing, all required documents are signed and delivered and funds are disbursed.

Commission.   The fee charged for an agent's services. Usually, but not always, the seller pays. There is no "set" fee; rather, the amount is fully negotiable.

Commitment.   A promise from lender to borrower offering a mortgage at a set amount, interest rate, and cost. Typically, commitments have a time limit; for example, they are good for 5 or 15 days. Some lenders charge for making a commitment if you don't subsequently take out the mortgage (since they have tied up the money for that amount of time). When the lender's offer is in writing, it is sometimes called a "firm commitment."

Conforming Loan.   A mortgage that conforms to the underwriting requirements of Fannie Mae or Freddie Mac.

Construction Loan.   A mortgage made for the purpose of constructing a building. The loan is short term, typically under 12 months, and is usually paid in installments directly to the builder as the work is completed. Most often, it is interest only.

Contingency.   A condition that limits a contract. For example, the most common contingency says that a buyer is not required to complete a purchase if he or she fails to get necessary financing. See also Subject To.

Conventional Loan.   Any loan that is not guaranteed or insured by the government.

Convertible Mortgage.   An adjustable-rate mortgage (ARM) with a clause allowing it to be converted to a fixed-rate mortgage at some time in the future. (Or sometimes the other way round.) You may have to pay an additional cost to obtain this type of mortgage.

Cosigner. Someone with better credit (usually a close relative) who agrees to sign your loan if you do not have good enough credit to qualify for a mortgage. The cosigner is equally responsible for repayment of the loan. (If you don't pay it back, the cosigner might be held liable for the entire balance.)

Credit Report. A report, usually from one of the country's three large credit reporting companies, that gives your credit history. It typically lists all your delinquent payments or failures to pay as well as any bankruptcies and, sometimes, foreclosures. Lenders use the report to determine whether to offer you a mortgage. The fee for obtaining the report is usually under $50, and you are often charged for it.

Deal Point. A point on which the deal hinges. It can be as important as the price or as trivial as changing the color of the mailbox.

Deposit. The money that buyers put up (also called "earnest money") to demonstrate their seriousness in making an offer. The deposit is usually at risk if the buyers fail to complete the transaction and have no acceptable way of backing out of the deal.

Disclosures. A list and explanation of features and defects in a property that sellers give to buyers. Most states now require disclosures.

Discount. The amount that a lender withholds from a mortgage to cover the points and fees. For example, you may borrow $100,000, but your points and fees come to $3,000; hence the lender will fund only $97,000, discounting the $3,000. Also, in the secondary market, a discount is the amount less than face value that a buyer of a mortgage pays in order to be induced to take out the loan. The discount here is calculated on the basis of risk, market rates, interest rate of the note, and other factors. See Points.

Dual Agent.   An agent who expresses loyalty to both buyers and sellers and agrees to work with both. Only a few agents can successfully play this role.

Due-on-Encumbrance Clause.   A little noted and seldom-enforced clause in recent mortgages that allows the lender to foreclose if the borrower gets additional financing.

For example, if you secure a second mortgage, the lender of the first mortgage may have grounds for foreclosing. The reasoning here is that if you reduce your equity level by taking out additional financing, the lender may be placed in a less secure position.

Due-on-Sale Clause.   A clause in a mortgage specifying that the entire unpaid balance becomes due and payable on sale of the property. See Acceleration Clause.

Escrow Company.   An independent party (stakeholder) that handles funds; carries out the instructions of the lender, buyer, and seller in a transaction; and deals with all the documents. In most states, companies are licensed to handle escrows. In some parts of the country, particularly the Northeast, the function of the escrow company may be handled by an attorney.

Fannie Mae.   Any of the publicly traded securities collateralized by a pool of mortgages backed by the Federal National Mortgage Association. A secondary lender.

FHA Loan.   A mortgage insured by the Federal Housing Administration. In most cases, the FHA advances no money, but instead insures the loan to a lender such as a bank.

There is a fee to the borrower, usually paid up front, for this insurance.

Fixed-Rate Mortgage.   A mortgage whose interest rate does not fluctuate for the life of the loan.

Fixer-Upper.   A home that does not show well and is in bad shape. Often the property is euphemistically referred to in listings as a "TLC" (needs tender loving care) or "handyman's special."

Foreclosure.   Legal proceeding in which the lender takes possession of and title to a property, usually after the borrower fails to make timely payments on a mortgage.

Freddie Mac.   A publicly traded security collateralized by a pool of mortgages backed by the Federal Home Loan Mortgage Corporation, a secondary lender.

FSBO.   A property that is "For Sale By Owner."

Garbage Fees.   Extra (and often unnecessary) charges tacked on by the lender when a buyer obtains a mortgage.

Graduated-Payment Mortgage.   A mortgage whose payments vary over the life of the loan. They start out low, then slowly rise until, usually after a few years, they reach a plateau where they remain for the balance of the term. Such a mortgage is particularly useful when you want low initial payments. It is primarily used by first-time buyers, often in combination with a fixed-rate or adjustable-rate mortgage.

Growing Equity Mortgage.   A rarely used mortgage whose payments increase according to a set schedule. The purpose is to pay additional money into principal and thus pay off the loan earlier and save interest charges.

HOA (Homeowners Association).   An organization found mainly in condos but also in some single-family home areas. It represents homeowners and establishes and maintains neighborhood architectural and other standards. You usually must get permission from the HOA to make significant external changes to your property.

Index. A measurement of an established interest rate used to determine the periodic adjustments for adjustable-rate mortgages. There are a wide variety of indexes, including the Treasury bill rates and the cost of funds to lenders.

Inspection. A physical survey of the property to determine if there are any problems or defects.

Jumbo. A mortgage for more than the maximum amount of a Conforming Loan.

Lien. A claim for money against real estate. For example, if you had work done on your property and refused to pay the worker, he or she might file a "mechanic's lien" against your property. If you didn't pay taxes, the taxing agency might file a "tax lien." These liens "cloud" the title and usually prevent you from selling the property or refinancing it until they are cleared by paying off the debt.

Loan-to-Value Ratio (LTV). The percentage of the appraised value of a property that a lender will loan. For example, if your property appraises at $100,000 and the lender is willing to loan $80,000, the loan-to-value ratio is 80 percent.

Lock In. To tie up the interest rate for a mortgage in advance of actually getting it. For example, a buyer might "lock in" a mortgage at 6.5 percent so that if rates subsequently rose, he or she would still get that rate. Sometimes there's a fee for this. It's always a good idea to get it in writing from the lender just to be sure that if rates rise the lender doesn't change its mind.

Lowball.   To make a very low initial offer to purchase.

MAI   A designation indicating a member of the American Institute of Real Estate Appraisers. An appraiser with this designation has completed rigorous training.

Margin.   An amount, calculated in points, that a lender adds to an index to determine how much interest you will pay during a period for an adjustable-rate mortgage. For example, the index may be at 7 percent and the margin, agreed upon at the time you obtain the mortgage, may be 2.7 points. The interest rate for that period, therefore, is 9.7 percent. See also Index; Points.

Median Sales Price.   The midpoint of the price of homes—as many properties have sold above this price as have sold below it.

MLS (Multiple Listing Service).   Used by Realtors as a listings exchange. Nearly 90 percent of all homes listed in the country are found on the MLS.

Mortgage.   A loan arrangement between a borrower, or "mortgagor," and a lender, or "mortgagee." If you don't make your payments on a mortgage, the lender can foreclose, or take ownership of the property, only by going to court. This court action can take a great deal of time, often six months or more. Further, even after the lender has taken back the property, you may have an "equity of redemption" that allows you to redeem the property for years afterward by paying back the mortgage and the lender's costs.

The length of time it takes to foreclose, the costs involved, and the equity of redemption make a mortgage much less desirable to lenders than a Trust Deed.

Mortgage Banker.   A lender that specializes in offering mortgages but none of the other services normally provided by a bank.

Mortgage Broker. A company that specializes in providing "retail" mortgages to consumers. It usually represents many different lenders.

Motivated Seller. A seller who has a strong desire to sell. For example, the seller may have been transferred and must move quickly.

Multiple Counteroffers. Comeback offers extended by the seller to several buyers simultaneously.

Multiple Offers. Offers submitted simultaneously from several buyers for the same property.

Negative Amortization. A condition arising when the payment on an adjustable-rate mortgage is not sufficiently large to cover the interest charged. The excess interest is then added to the principal, so that the amount borrowed actually increases. With government backed loans, the amount that the principal can increase is usually limited to 125 percent of the original mortgage value. Any mortgage that includes payment caps has the potential to be negatively amortized.

Origination Fee. An expense in obtaining a mortgage. Originally, it was a charge that lenders made for preparing and submitting a mortgage. The fee applied only to FHA and VA loans, which had to be submitted to the government for approval. With an FHA loan, the maximum origination fee was 1 percent.

Personal Property. Any property that does not go with the land. Such property includes automobiles, clothing, and most furniture. Some items such as appliances and floor and wall coverings are disputable. See also Real Property.

PITI (principal, interest, taxes, and insurance). These are the major components that go into determining the monthly payment on a mortgage. (Other items include homeowner's dues and utilities.)

Points. A point is 1 percent of a mortgage amount, payable on obtaining the loan. For example, if your mortgage is $100,000 and you are required to pay $2\frac{1}{2}$ points to get it, the charge to you is $2\frac{1}{2}$ percent or $2,500. Some points may be tax deductible. Check with your accountant.

A "basis point" is $\frac{1}{100}$ of a point.

Preapproval. Formal approval for a mortgage from a lender. You have to submit a standard application and have a credit check. Also, the lender may require proof of income, employment, and money on deposit (to be used for the down payment and closing costs).

Prepayment Penalty. A charge demanded by the lender from the borrower for paying off a mortgage early. In times past (more than 25 years ago) nearly all mortgages carried prepayment penalties. However, those mortgages were also assumable by others. Today virtually no fixed-rate mortgages (other than FHA or VA mortgages) are truly assumable, however some carry a prepayment penalty clause. See Assumption.

Private Mortgage Insurance (PMI). Insurance that protects the lender in the event that the borrower defaults on a mortgage. It is written by an independent third-party insurance company and typically covers only the first 20 percent of the lender's potential loss. PMI is normally required on any mortgage that exceeds an 80 percent loan-to-value ratio.

Purchase Money Mortgage. A mortgage obtained as part of the purchase price of a home (usually from the seller), as opposed to a mortgage obtained through refinancing.

In some states, no deficiency judgment can be obtained against the borrower of a purchase money mortgage. (That is, if there is a foreclosure and the property brings less than the amount borrowed, the borrower cannot be held liable for the shortfall.)

Real Property. Real estate is real property. This includes the land and anything appurtenant to it, including the house. Certain tests have been devised to determine whether an item is real property (goes with the land). For example, if curtains or drapes have been attached in such a way that they cannot be removed without damaging the home, they may be spoken of as real property. On the other hand, if they can easily be removed without damaging the home, they may be personal property. The purchase agreement should specify whether doubtful items are real or personal to avoid confusion later on.

Realtor® A broker who is a member of the National Association of Realtors. Agents who are not members may not use the Realtor designation.

REO (real estate owned). A term that refers to property taken back through foreclosure and held for sale by a lender.

RESPA (Real Estate Settlement Procedures Act). Legislation requiring lenders to provide borrowers with specified information on the cost of securing financing. Basically it means that before you proceed far along the path of getting the mortgage, the lender has to provide you with an estimate of costs. Then, before you sign the documents binding you to the mortgage, the lender has to provide you with a breakdown of the actual costs.

Second Mortgage.   An inferior mortgage usually placed on the property after a first mortgage. In the event of foreclosure, the second mortgage is paid off only if and when the first mortgage has been fully paid. Many lenders will not offer second mortgages.

Short Sale.   Property sale in which a lender agrees to accept less than the mortgage amount in order to facilitate the sale and avoid a foreclosure.

SREA (Society of Real Estate Appraisers).   A professional association to which qualified appraisers can belong.

Subject To.   A phrase often used to indicate that a buyer is not assuming the mortgage liability of a seller. For example, if the seller has an assumable loan and you (the buyer) "assume" the loan, you are taking over liability for payment. On the other hand, if you purchase "subject to" the mortgage, you do not assume liability for payment.

Subordination Clause.   A clause in a mortgage document that keeps the mortgage subordinate to another mortgage.

Title.   Legal evidence that you actually have the right of ownership of Real Property. It is given in the form of a deed (there are many different types of deeds) that specifies the kind of title you have (joint, common, or other).

Title Insurance Policy.   An insurance policy that covers the title to a home. It may list the owner or the lender as beneficiary. The policy is issued by a title insurance company and specifies that if for any covered reason your title proves defective, the company will correct the title or compensate you up to a specified amount, usually the amount of the purchase price or the mortgage. (The coverage is "backwards"—normally covering the time up until the policy was issued.)

Trust Deed.   A three-party lending arrangement that includes a borrower, or "trustor"; an independent third-party stakeholder, or "trustee" (usually a title insurance company); and a lender, or "beneficiary" so-called because the lender stands to benefit if the borrower fails to make payments. The advantage of the trust deed over the mortgage is that foreclosure can be accomplished without court action. No deficiency judgment against the borrower, then, is allowed. (In other words, if the property is worth less than the loan, the lender usually can't come back to the borrower after the sale for the difference.) See also Purchase Money Mortgage.

Upgrade.   Any extra that a buyer may obtain when purchasing a new home—for example, a better-quality carpet or a wall mirror in the bedroom.

Upside Down.   Owing more on a property than its market value.

VA Loan.   A mortgage guaranteed by the Department of Veterans Affairs. The VA actually guarantees only a small percentage of the loan amount, but since it guarantees the "top" of the monies loaned, lenders are willing to accept the arrangement. In a VA loan the government advances no money; rather, the mortgage is made by a private lender such as a bank.

Wraparound Financing.   A blend of two mortgages, often used by commerical property sellers to get a higher interest rate or facilitate a sale. For example, instead of giving a buyer a simple *Second Mortgage*, the seller may combine the balance due on an existing mortgage (usually an existing first) with an additional loan. Thus the wrap includes both the second and the first mortgages. The borrower makes payments to the seller, who then keeps part of the payment and in turn pays off the existing mortgage.

What You Should Know about Mortgages

For most people, the first consideration with regard to a mortgage is the interest rate. Higher interest rates translate into higher payments; lower rates, lower payments. Consequently, most people just want the lowest interest rates possible.

TRAP

The best way to compare interest rates is to do it for *like-kind* mortgages. You don't want to compare apples and oranges. Today there are two major kinds of conventional (nongovernment insured or guaranteed) mortgages available: a fixed-rate mortgage, where the interest rate does not change for the life of the loan, and an adjustable-rate mortgage, where the interest rate can change. When you compare mortgages, be sure you compare fixed-rate to fixed-rate and adjustable to adjustable. (There are so many different varieties of adjustable-rate mortgages that comparing them is really very difficult.) Of course, at some point, you'll also want to compare adjustable with fixed, but that's a much more complex calculation, as we'll see shortly.

If you have a credit blemish or have trouble otherwise qualifying, shop for a lender, not an interest rate. Some lenders specialize in borrowers with problems; others won't touch them.

How to Compare New Fixed-Rate Mortgages

Each lender who offers fixed-rate mortgages posts its current interest rate. These rates are often printed weekly in local papers. They also can change daily. In many areas a newsletter or online service gathers them all up and sends them off to agents.

Adjustable-interest-rate mortgages always offer lower rates. But the adjustable rate will rise when the interest rate market goes up. It's usually better to lock in a fixed-rate mortgage when the interest rate market is low, than to try for an extra point or so by getting an adjustable rate.

There are also numerous online lenders such as eloan.com and quickenloan.com that post current interest rates. These are very easy to check simply by going to their Web sites. Major online services such as MSN.com and bankrate.com will also lead you to mortgage rate postings.

But best of all, if you check with a mortgage broker who handles dozens of lenders, he or she can quickly tell you the best rate in town for the specific amount and type of loan you're hunting for. See Table A.1 for what a typical list of lenders might look like.

What's the best loan in the list? It's the best combination of interest rates, points, and fees. In Table A.1, Amalgamated's loan

TABLE A.1 Making the Fixed-Rate Comparison

LENDER	INTEREST RATE	POINTS	FEES
Associated Lenders	6.7	0.0	0
ABC S&L	6.4	1.5	1,400
Amalgamated Bank	6.3	0.5	700
Jones Bankers	6.2	2.5	1,350
WW S&L	6.1	3.0	1,200

is outstanding because of the low interest rate, low points, and few fees, even though Jones and WW offer a lower interest rate.

At first glance, this list of interest rates might seem complex. After all, there isn't just an interest rate. There are also "points" and "fees." What's that all about?

What Are Points?

A point is a single percentage of a mortgage. Thus 2 points on a $100,000 loan equals 2 percent, or $2,000; 4 points equals 4 percent, or $4,000; and so forth.

Points are a trade off the lender is making. If you want a lower interest rate loan (lower than the market), you can get it, if you're willing to pay points. The more points you pay, the lower the interest rate will be.

On the other hand, since points are cash out of your pocket, you may be willing to accept a higher interest rate. The higher the rate, the fewer the points. Normally at zero points, you're paying the market rate.

NOTE The interest rate is very important since it will help determine your monthly payment. The higher the interest rate, the higher your payment will be; the lower the interest rate, the lower your payment.

What Are Mortgage Fees?

Another charge or costs are "loan fees." These can be almost any amount from nothing (where the fees are absorbed into a higher loan amount or higher interest rate) to many thousands of dollars. While some lenders are very up front about telling you what these fees are, some sneak them in at the last moment.

When the loan fees are simply added on to give the lender a better "yield" (total return on the mortgage), they are called "garbage fees."

If you are primarily interested in the lowest monthly payment and have some cash on hand, look for the lowest interest rate. However, be aware that lenders with low interest rates often make up for it by jacking up the points. It may cost you some cash to get the loan.

On the other hand, if you want to reduce your closing costs and can stand a bit higher monthly payment, look for a lender who charges few to no closing costs and points. You'll usually pay a higher interest rate, but you won't have to come up with as much cash out of pocket.

TRAP

In all cases, if the interest rate or closing costs are unreasonably high, seek another lender. But do this when you first apply, so you have time to change. If you wait until the deal is ready to close, it may be too late to go hunting for a new lender.

TIP

Many lenders today will allow you to trade closing costs and points for interest rates. They'll even have a scale. As the interest rate goes up, the closing and points go down and vice versa. (See Table A.1.) Be sure you compare lenders here. Sometimes you'll find that the trade-offs are too steep from one lender, but much more reasonable from another.

How to Compare Adjustable-Rate Mortgages

Adjustable-rate mortgages (ARMs) can also be compared, except that many more factors are involved. The first thing you'll notice is that the interest rates usually will seem much lower for ARMs than for fixed-rate loans. Once again, don't be fooled. Remember, compare apples with apples, not apples with oranges.

The low initial interest rate (often called the "teaser") is the traditional appeal of ARMs. As such, they appear to be giving you a better deal. But it isn't necessarily so.

There are a number of different factors to take into account when comparing adjustable-rate mortgages. We'll cover six of the most important:

- Teaser rate
- Caps
- Steps
- Adjustment period
- Indexes
- Margin

What Is a Teaser Rate?

Most ARMs have a low beginning interest rate. This is usually only a "teaser," a come-on to get you to sign up for the ARM. Often the teaser is several percentage points below the true rate. What this means is that in the first few adjustment periods, your effective interest rate will rise even if interest rates in general do not!

As an example, the discounted teaser rate may be 4 percent and the true market rate may be 7. You get the ARM at 4 percent. However, if it has three-month adjustment periods with a maximum adjustment of 1 percent in interest each period, within nine months it will be up to 7 percent. Your interest rate will go up 1 percent the first three-month period, 1 percent the second three-month period, and 1 percent the third three-month period, so that nine months after you get the loan you are paying 7 percent instead of 4.

Additionally, some of these loans are written in such a way that the interest rate will continue on up to make up for the below market interest rate you received as part of the teaser. So your interest rate could continue on up beyond 7 percent for a time!

Remember, the teaser rate is only temporary. Don't be fooled into thinking that it is the true rate of your mortgage.

Ask the lender what the true rate is. You'll be shown the APR (annual percentage rate), which will be higher than the teaser but probably still not as high as the current market rate of the mortgage (because the APR is a blending of the teaser and the current mortgage rate).

When comparing ARMs, it's usually to your advantage to go for the one where the teaser *lasts the longest*, thus maximizing your period of low interest rates.

What Are Caps?

Adjustable rates often have caps limiting the maximum amount that the interest rate can rise over the term of the loan and the adjustment period. Rate caps prevent the interest rate on an adjustable-rate mortgage from rising indefinitely.

Some loans offer "payment caps," where the amount the monthly payment can rise (to compensate for a rising interest rate) is also capped. It sounds like a good idea, but in reality it can be a trap. Monthly payment caps often lead to "negative amortization," which, simply put, means that you end up owing much more than you originally borrowed!

Negative amortization happens when the interest rate goes up and your monthly payment does not. In this case, each month you may not be paying enough to meet just the interest on the mortgage, let alone repaying the principal.

The excess interest is then added to the principal and you end up paying more than you originally borrowed! (Usually on government-backed mortgages the lender cannot increase the principal of the mortgage over 125 percent of its original amount through negative amortization.)

What Are Steps?

Steps are the maximum amount the interest rate can rise (or fall) during any one adjustment period. For example, a 1.5 step means that the maximum amount the interest rate can vary during the adjustment period is 1.5 percent. Generally speaking, most borrowers prefer shorter steps when interest rates are rising.

However, if the steps are too short to fully accommodate the market's interest rate increase, many loans provide that the excess can be carried over to the next adjustment period.

What's an Adjustment Period?

This is the time between which rate adjustments can be made. Adjust periods vary between a short of one month and a long of three years or more. Generally speaking, most borrowers like a longer adjustment period when rates are rising, a shorter one when they are falling.

For example, see Table A.2 for a summary of what different lenders' caps might look like.

TABLE A.2 Comparing Arms

LENDER	INTEREST RATE	STEPS	ADJUSTMENT PERIOD	CAP
AVD S&L	5.00	1	6 months	5
Mary's Bank	4.50	2	3 months	6
City S&L	3.78	1	monthly	8

For AVD S&L the teaser rate is 5 percent. It can rise 1 percent every six-month adjustment period with a cap of 5 percent to a total of 10 percent.

For Mary's Bank the teaser rate is a lower 4.5 percent. However, it can rise faster, 2 percent every three-month adjustment period with a 6 percent cap to a total of 10.5 percent.

City S&L offers the lowest teaser, 3.78 percent. However, the rate can rise the fastest, 1 percent every month up to a cap of 8 percent, or a total interest rate of nearly 12 percent.

Note that while City S&L appears to have the lowest interest rate, because of the short adjustment period that rate can rise faster than the rate of any of the other lenders, who apparently have higher teaser rates but longer adjustment periods.

TRAP

Be careful not to look at just the teaser rate. Check also the steps, adjustment period, and the caps. These all help to determine how fast the interest rate and, consequently, the monthly payments on the loan go up.

In addition to an initial low teaser interest rate, in general, to get the longest teaser term, you want to avoid payment caps and look for the lowest interest rate cap combined with the shortest steps and longest adjustment period. This should maximize the amount of time your teaser will last.

What Are ARM Indexes?

Adjustable-rate mortgages are all tied to interest rate indexes that are independent of the lenders. These indexes rise and fall along with other interest rates and, accordingly, so does the rate on your mortgage. Ideally, most borrowers want an interest rate that has the least volatility so your mortgage payment won't bounce around too much. On the other hand, lenders want a more volatile interest rate that more closely corresponds to the changes in the marketplace.

Most Commonly Used Indexes

- 6-month T-bill rate
- 1-year T-bill rate
- 3-year T-bill rate
- Libor index (London Interbank Offered Rate)
- Cost of funds for the lender
- Average of fixed-rate mortgages
- Average rate paid on jumbo CDs

Lenders should provide you with a chart showing changes in the index for your loan. Be sure you ask for a chart that includes the period of 1979 through 1981 and 1999 to 2003 so you can see how the index performed in both high-interest-rate and low-interest-rate economic conditions.

What Is the Margin?

Each adjustable rate has a margin. This is a figure that is added to the index to give you your interest rate. For example, the margin might be 3 percent. Thus, if the index is at 5 percent, add the 3 percent margin and you have your effective mortgage interest rate of 8 percent.

TRAP

Keep in mind that the index rate is not your interest rate. The lender's margin is added to the index, this can increase your effective interest rate by 2 to 5 percent or more.

Plan Your Strategy

If you're going to live in the home only a short time and then resell, get the lowest teaser rate with the longest adjustment periods and shortest steps possible. For example, if you plan to live in the property for only three years, you might be able to find an ARM that gives you a below-market interest rate for the entire period of time!

Also, most people aim for the most stable index. That way you have a better idea of your monthly payments. But if interest rates are falling, you may want a more volatile index that will reflect falling rates in a falling monthly payment.

In addition, don't compare just interest rates and points with ARMs. Sometimes an ARM with a higher interest rate and more points is a better deal, if it has a more favorable adjustment period, steps, margin, and so on.

Comparing Adjustable-Rate with Fixed-Rate Mortgages

Now we're at the stage of comparing apples with oranges. However, in truth, a direct one-to-one comparison isn't usually very helpful. Rather, what's more important to most borrowers is comparing the usefulness of each type. It's sort of like saying, "Do I want to eat an orange now, or will an apple taste better?" Here are some guidelines that may prove helpful.

When interest rates are low, get a fixed-rate mortgage and lock in the low rate. When interest rates are high, consider an adjustable-rate mortgage with payments that will fall as interest rates come down.

If you desperately want to buy a home but can't qualify for a fixed-rate mortgage, try an adjustable. The lower teaser rate should make qualifying a bit easier. (Currently lenders qualify not just on the basis of the teaser, but on an average between the market rate and the teaser, which is still probably lower than for a comparable fixed-rate mortgage.)

If you can't afford to have fluctuations in your monthly payment, get a fixed-rate mortgage. You'll at least know what your payments will be every month.

If you plan to sell soon, get an ARM and take advantage of the low teaser rate. But beware, your plans could change unexpectedly!

Sometimes ARMs have lower initial loan costs. If cash is a big consideration for you, look into them. Remember that with an ARM, if interest rates go up, so do your payments. (This may occur even after rates have peaked and started to come down. Because of your adjustment period, you may play "catch-up" for months after the downturn.) You can't call your lender later and say, "I can't handle a $200 increase in my monthly payment!" Your lender isn't going to be sympathetic and will threaten you with foreclosure if you don't pay. The time to consider a big monthly increase is before you get that adjustable-rate mortgage, not afterward.

Fixed- or Adjustable-Rate Mortgage?

You should get a fixed-rate mortgage:

- So you can lock in a low-interest rate.
- If you plan on keeping the property a long time.

- If you want a fixed mortgage payment (does not go up or down).

You should get an adjustable-rate mortgage:

- If interest rates are high and you can get a long-term, low initial (teaser) rate.
- If you plan on selling or refinancing soon.
- If you can handle flexible mortgage payments (that can rise during the life of the loan).

Hybrids—What About a Combination Fixed and Adjustable?

There are a whole bunch of hybrids out there, any one of which may be better for your situation than a straight fixed or ARM mortgage.

What Is a Convertible Mortgage?

Some ARMs may be "convertible" to a fixed rate, or vice versa. Many allow a conversion at a set date—three or seven years, for example—in the future. Just be sure the conversion is guaranteed at the lowest interest rate at the time of conversion.

There are literally hundreds of types of convertible mortgages available. Some lenders will even create one just to suit your financial situation. Be sure to ask.

What About Short-Term Fixed, Amortized over 30 Years

The whole point behind an ARM, from a lender's perspective, is to give a loan that can respond to interest rate fluctuations. Another way of accomplishing this is to give a shorter-term fixed-rate mortgage.

Currently lenders are offering short-term fixed-rate mortgages in the following time lengths, all amortized over 30 years: 15 years, 10 years, 7 years, 5 years, or 3 years. The shorter the term, the better the interest rate is. What this means is that after the initial period, you have a "balloon," a single large payment where the remaining balance is due.

For example, you can get an interest rate reduction if you agree to get a loan that pays off in full in 15 years (see the following section). You might get an even bigger reduction if you agree to a balloon in 5 years instead of a full payoff in 30. If you agree to a balloon in 3, you might get the interest rate reduced the most. (*Note*: The monthly payments are still spread out—amortized—on the basis of 30 years. It's just that you have a shorter due date, or balloon payment at the end.)

TRAP

On short-term fixed-rate mortgages, if it turns out that you can't sell or refinance as you planned at the end of the term, you could lose the property to foreclosure! You're gambling a lower interest rate on future market and personal financial conditions. Therefore, make sure a shorter-term mortgage includes an automatic refinancing option at the end. Usually this is an ugly adjustable, but at least if worse comes to worst, you won't be without a loan.

Hybrid mortgages are available from banks, savings institutions, and mortgage brokers—anywhere that you'd get any other type of mortgage. However, your best sources are the mortgage brokers, who deal with many lenders and, thus, have a better sense of what's out there.

Balloon or Amortize (Spread Out) Payments?

You should get a balloon mortgage:

- If you plan on reselling or refinancing soon.
- If you need a lower interest rate.

- If you can lock in a "roll-over" loan to cover the balloon when it comes due.

You should get a fully amortized mortgage:

- If you want equal payments to fully pay off the loan.
- If you plan on keeping the property a long time.
- If the risk of a big balloon payment (or having to take out a high-interest roll-over loan) doesn't bother you.

What About a Fully Amortized 15-Year Mortgage?

Some people simply want a shorter mortgage. As opposed to the hybrids just discussed, in a fully amortized shorter-term mortgage, the payments are higher so it can be fully paid off at the end of, say, 15 years. (With a hybrid, you have lower payments, but a balloon at the end—here the mortgage is paid completely in equal installments for the term of the mortgage.)

The advantage here is much less interest over time. With a 30-year amortized mortgage the total interest is more than twice as much at the same interest rate than with a 15-year fully amortized mortgage! Of course, you may be saying to yourself that this is all well and good—yes, you save more than half the interest. But you probably more than double your payments.

Not quite. The difference in payments between the same 15-year and 30-year mortgages is only about 20 percent. You'll end up paying only about 20 percent more monthly. (Yes, it really does work out that way. It's all in the way mortgages are calculated.)

Many people like the idea of saving interest, and since they currently have enough income, they jump to a 15-year mortgage. The problem is the higher monthly payment. What if at some point during the time you're paying back the mortgage, you get ill or lose your job? It's a lot harder to repay a higher monthly payment than a lower one.

The solution is to get a 30-year mortgage with no prepayment penalty. (Most modern mortgages don't have penalties for early repayment.) No prepayment penalty means that you can pay a higher monthly payment at any time you want. Thus, you can pay the extra monthly amount to turn a 30-year loan into a 15. However, if the loan was originally set up as a 30-year, then if at any time making that higher payment becomes a hardship, you can drop back to the lower 30-year payment. When things get better, you again pay more.

Here, you get the advantage of being able to pay off the mortgage in a short time *if you choose*, but also have the safety of a lower payment if hard times hit.

What About Biweekly Payments?

Popular a few years ago, some biweekly mortgages are still around. Here, instead of paying your mortgage each month, you pay half the monthly amount every other week. The result is that you actually pay an extra month each year. (There are 12 months, but 52 weeks in a year, meaning you would make 26 biweekly payments, which equals 13 months.) Over the long haul, that extra month means you end up paying more in principal each year, which means much less interest down the road. This works for either a 30-year or a 15-year mortgage. With a 30-year mortgage, going biweekly can mean paying it off in around 23 years.

The problem with biweekly mortgages is that you can be forever writing checks. Therefore, the only realistic way of handling them is to have the money taken out of your account automatically every two weeks. You can easily set this up yourself at your bank, or for a hefty fee, there are service companies that will do it for you.

Keep in mind, however, the biweekly mortgage is not for someone who is self-employed and gets paid irregularly. An unstable cash flow can cause real problems when you have a mortgage payment due every other week.

What About FHA or VA Loans?

The government, except in some rare instances, does not lend mortgage money directly to consumers. It does, however, insure or guarantee lenders, who thus are willing to give you a mortgage, oftentimes at better than conventional nongovernment rates.

What Is the FHA Program?

FHA mortgages are insured by the government and are offered through most lenders, such as banks and S&Ls. Generally the down payment is low, around 3 percent. The interest rate, however, is usually competitive with conventional loans. Recently the ceiling for FHA loans was expanded to a much higher amount than in the past—check with a good mortgage lender for the current maximum loan.

If you get a new FHA loan, you'll have to pay the insurance premium for the loan up front. (See the explanation for the similar PMI in Chapter 18.) The premium is fairly high—close to 4 percent of the loan amount. You can, however, add the premium to the loan, although this does increase your monthly payments.

Additionally, you are required to occupy the property as your residence in order to get a low down payment, and the property itself must pass a strict qualifying appraisal.

There are generally no prepayment penalties for FHA mortgages and they are partially assumable. (That means that the buyers must qualify as if they were getting a new FHA loan. However, generally they can assume the seller's loan at the existing interest rate.)

What Is the Veterans Program?

Some loans are guaranteed by the Department of Veterans Affairs (VA). The guarantee is not to you, but to the bank or S&L that makes the loan. These mortgages offer competitive interest rates and, in many cases, no down payments and reduced closing costs.

In order to get a VA loan you must have been on the active list in the armed forces during certain periods of time. (These change periodically. Check with the Department of Veterans Affairs for the current requirements at www.va.gov.) In addition, the property must pass a rigorous appraisal. Finally, you must plan to occupy the property.

VA loans are usually nothing down to you and the seller must pay most of the closing costs. Further, in general, they are fully assumable. You can sell the property and the buyers can pick up the loan at the existing interest rate. However, once you get a VA loan, you are on the hook for that loan for as long as it is on the property. Even if at some later date you sell the property, you may still be responsible for the loan! If the future buyer defaults, the VA could come looking to you for repayment! You must get a release of responsibility from the VA at the time someone else buys to fully get off the hook. (But that next buyer must then qualify as a veteran.)

What Is a Graduated-Payment Loan?

Less popular today than in the past, loans with a graduated (instead of fixed) payment can be incorporated with almost any other, including government loans. Generally it means that you pay less when you first get the loan and are least able to pay. Then, presumably as your income goes up, so does the monthly payment.

Don't get a graduated-payment loan unless you're quite certain you're going to have an increase in income. If your income remains the same or declines, you could be in big trouble down the road.

What About Reverse-Equity (Annuity) Mortgages?

After a halting start over a decade ago, reverse-equity mortgages are making a comeback. Designed for senior citizens, they allow you to live in your house and get a monthly stipend from a mortgage you put on it. The amount that you receive is added to the mortgage amount each month, plus interest. You can stay in the house until you die; then the lender gets the place and can resell. The FHA provides probably the most fair of these mortgages.

TRAP

If you're looking at a reverse-equity mortgage, be sure the loan provides that you can live in the property in perpetuity. You wouldn't want to be evicted after a dozen years or so because the mortgage had grown higher than the value of the property. Again, check out this feature in an FHA version.

Very few lenders offer reverse-equity loans. Consult with a mortgage broker about possible sources in your area.

Should You Ask the Sellers for a Second Mortgage?

If the sellers are willing, it's probably the best mortgage you can get. There's usually no qualifying and you can bargain for the interest rate. (You might offer a slightly higher purchase price for a lower interest rate.)

Many sellers, however, cannot give a second mortgage because they need to cash out in order to buy another home. Others are reluctant, fearing you might not make the payments and they would have the considerable expense of foreclosing and taking the property back.

You can also get a second mortgage from an institutional lender such as a bank. Here the second mortgage typically has a higher interest rate than the first.

Watch out for "balloon payments" on seconds. This results when the mortgage is not fully amortized—when the monthly payments do not fully pay off the principal. At the end of the term on a seller's second, you could end up owing a substantial amount of money. For example, if you borrow $10,000 at 10 percent, interest only, for seven years, at the end of the term, you still owe $10,000! (It was *interest only!*)

Of course, seconds can be amortized, or paid off monthly.

However, many seconds have payments which only partially return all the principal. This is frequently the case with a mortgage that is "amortized for 15 years, due in 5," which is similar to the short-term fixed-rate loans discussed earlier.

This means that the monthly payment is high enough to pay back the loan in 15 years. But you owe it all back in 5 years. When the fifth year comes around, most of your principal is still owing. Now you must either dig deep into your pockets or refinance.

What Are Discount/Prepayment Mortgages?

More recently entering the market are discount/prepayment loans. These typically offer you a discount on the interest rate in the form of cash back *if* you agree not to pay off (prepay) the mortgage for a set period of time. For example, the lender may offer you a $1,000 discount provided you won't prepay within three years. If, however, for whatever reason you must prepay before the time limit, you are subject to a hefty penalty, sometimes six months' worth of interest.

To many people this sounds great. The lender is paying you when you get the mortgage. However, it could be a poor bonus if your fortunes turn and you suddenly need to refinance. If you do, the penalty could hurt. In most cases, there is no penalty if you sell instead of refinancing during the prepayment phase of the loan.

TRAP

Beware of lenders who offer a very low incentive discount, a very long prepayment period, and a high penalty. You could end up being locked in for five years just to save 500 bucks, with thousands in penalties for prepaying.

Discount/prepayment loans are available from banks, savings and loans, and mortgage brokers on most types of mortgages, including both fixed and adjustable.

Important Internet Resources

Robert Irwin (www.robertirwin.com) The author's Web site

Government Agencies

Housing and Urban Development (www.hud.gov) Information on government programs including those involving settlement/closing procedures

Federal Housing Administration (www.hud.gov/offices/hsg/index.cfm) Information on FHA loan insurance and housing programs

Department of Veterans Affairs (www.va.gov) Information on VA loan guarantees and housing programs

Secondary Lenders

Fannie Mae (www.fanniemae.com and www.homepath.com) Information on loans, settlement procedures, and foreclosures

Freddie Mac (www.freddiemac.com) Information on loans and settlement procedures

Ginnie Mae (www.ginniemae.gov) Information on home purchasing and ownership

Credit Bureaus and Organizations

Free Annual Credit Reports (www.annualcreditreport.com) Obtain a free credit report from each of the three credit bureaus once a year

Equifax (www.equifax.com) National credit reporting agency

Experian (www.experian.com) National credit reporting agency

Fair Isaac (credit scores) (www.fairisaac.com) Main credit scoring organization

Federal Trade Commission (www.ftc.gov) Handles credit reporting complaints

TransUnion (www.transunion.com) National credit reporting agency

Title Insurance/Escrow Organizations

ALTA form (www.alta.org/forms) Provides the basic form for ALTA policies

American Escrow Association (www.a-e-a.org) Major escrow trade association

American Land Title Associations (www.alta.org) A major title association trade association

California Escrow Association (www.ceaescrow.org) California trade escrow association

California Land Title Association (www.alta.org/store/forms/home own.pdf) California trade title association

Chicago Title Insurance Company (www.ctic.com) Major independent title insurance company

First American Title Insurance Company (www.firstam.com) Major independent title insurance company

Illinois Land Title Association (www.illinoislandtitle.org) Illinois trade title insurance association

Texas Land Title Association (www.tlta.com) Texas trade title insurance association

Title Vest (www.titlevest.com) Online title insurance

Home Inspection Organizations

American Institute of Inspectors (www.inspection.org) Home inspection trade association

American Society of Home Inspectors (www.ashi.com) National home inspection trade association

National Association of Certified Home Inspectors (www. nachi.org) National home inspector trade association that certifies inspectors

Other Related Organizations

Dataquick (www.dataquick.com) Provides information on real estate (fee)

Foreclosure.com (www.foreclosure.com) Provides information on foreclosures

The Legal Description (www.thelegaldescription.com) Provides information on legal news regarding home closings

National Association of Realtors (www.realtor.org) Provides information on members, homes for sale, and other data

National Association of Realtors listings (www.realtor.com) Provides virtually all MLS listings nationwide

Realty Trac (www.realtytrac.com) Provides information on foreclosures

Index

About the Author

Robert Irwin is one of America's foremost experts in every area of real estate. He is the author of McGraw-Hill's bestselling Tips and Traps series, as well as *The Home Buyer's Checklist, How to Get Started in Real Estate Investing,* and *How to Buy a Home When You Can't Afford It.* His books have sold more than one million copies. Visit his Web site at www.robertirwin.com.